W9-DAH-368

Private Diplomacy
with the Soviet Union

The Institute for the Study of Diplomacy concentrates on the processes of conducting foreign relations abroad, in the belief that diplomatic skills can be taught or improved and that the case study method is useful to that end. *Working closely with the academic program of the Georgetown University School of Foreign Service, the Institute conducts a program of publication, teaching, research, conferences and lectures. An associates program enables experienced practitioners of international relations to conduct individual research while sharing their firsthand experience with the university community. Special programs include the junior fellowships in diplomacy, the Dean and Virginia Rusk midcareer fellowship, the Edward Weintal journalism prize, the Jit Trainor diplomacy award, and the Martin F. Herz monograph prize.*

The Institute gratefully acknowledges the
support of this volume by
The Exxon Education Foundation
and
The J. Howard Pew Freedom Trust

Private
Diplomacy
with the
Soviet Union

Edited by

David D. Newsom

INSTITUTE FOR THE
STUDY OF DIPLOMACY

UNIVERSITY
PRESS OF
AMERICA

LANHAM • NEW YORK • LONDON

GEORGETOWN UNIVERSITY

Copyright © 1987 by
The Institute for the Study of Diplomacy
Georgetown University
Washington, D.C. 20057
All rights reserved

University Press of America,® Inc.

4720 Boston Way
Lanham, MD 20706

3 Henrietta Street
London WC2E 8LU England

Printed in the United States of America

British Cataloging in Publication Information Available

Co-published by arrangement with
The Institute for the Study of Diplomacy,
Georgetown University

Library of Congress Cataloging in Publication Data

Private diplomacy with the Soviet Union.

    Contents: Introduction/ David D. Newsom — Nonofficial
exchanges with the Soviet Union / Walter J. Stoessel, Jr.
— Informal diplomacy, the Dartmouth Conference experi-
ence / Philip D. Stewart — [etc.]
    1. United States—Relations—Soviet Union.   2. Soviet
Union—Relations—United States.   3. Diplomats—United
States.   4. Diplomats—Soviet Union.   I. Newsom, David D.
II. Georgetown University.   Institute for the Study
of Diplomacy.
E183.8.S65P76   1987   327.73047   86-28926
ISBN 0-8191-5820-8 (alk. paper)
ISBN 0-8191-5821-6 (pbk. : alk. paper)

All University Press of America books are produced on acid-free
paper which exceeds the minimum standards set by the National
Historical Publication and Records Commission.

Contents

Introduction

David D. Newsom

O N THE SURFACE there would appear to be no more significant set of exchanges than those between citizens of the United States and of the Soviet Union. The handbook of the Institute for Soviet-American Relations identifies at least two hundred sixteen nongovernmental organizations in the United States that are involved in conferences and exchanges with Soviet counterparts or related public education activities.* In the ensuing essays of this monograph, the Institute for the Study of Diplomacy seeks to examine the value to the participants and to the basic relationship between the United States and the Soviet Union of such meetings between ostensibly private citizens of both countries.

This publication leans heavily on the experience of the Dartmouth group, the oldest in terms of experience of any of those listed. The experience of others, however, is also included. In addition, I have endeavored through conversations with those not represented in this publication further to broaden our insight into this subject.

Some of those involved in such private exchanges have been reluctant to set down their impressions through an understandable concern at the impact particularly negative or questioning comments might have on future possibilities of

---

The Handbook on Organizations Involved in Soviet-American Relations (Washington, DC: Institute for Soviet-American Relations, June 1986).

talks with the Soviets. Some have reported their experiences through other publications. We have reprinted two such reports.

Private exchanges between the citizens of the two super-powers, in our view, represent a significant part of the diplomacy between these nations. In the essays in this volume we have sought to have the writers express views on the degree to which these private exchanges give signals to the respective governments and through such signals have an impact on the basic political relationship and the policies of the two countries.

Some of the groups involved in these exchanges include delegations of those from the principal foreign policy circles and principal universities of the United States, including many former officials. There are other exchanges by those without such official experience or connection who see in citizen diplomacy an opportunity to convey the broad interest of the people of the United States in peaceful relations with the Soviet Union. The concentration of our monograph is on the former group.

Inevitably, the question arises in addressing the value of such exchanges, who gains? Responding to this, it is first necessary to ask why the citizens of each country are interested in such meetings.

The interest of the Soviet citizens remains a matter of conjecture. As one of the essays points out, there is a clear desire "to plug into ruling circles." What is less clear is whether the purpose of such contacts is merely to confirm an unshakable view of how policy is made in the United States, to look for knowledge about the United States, or to seek channels that will persuade, ultimately, the United States government of the seriousness of the Soviet position. What is clear from some of the essays and from speaking with those involved in the process is that the Soviets are always interested not only in who will be a member of such delegations, but whom they represent. Landrum Bolling in his essay points out the importance that the Soviets attach to the presence of David Rockefeller in the delegation of the Dartmouth group. Does this suggest that the Soviets believe their theories about the influence of such large private families as the Rockefellers on total U.S. policy?

The gains for the United States are also difficult to evaluate fully. As Walter Stoessel points out in his essay, these exchanges do sometimes provide insights into Soviet policy and "nuances" that supplement what is heard in official channels. None of those writing or discussing this question with us, however, suggest that Soviet participants depart very far from the Soviet official position. What participants do emphasize is the importance of corridor talks and the degree to which, over time, those involved in such exchanges build a wider circle of relationships and contacts in the Soviet Union and an increasing credibility within such circles.

There are clearly many problems and limitations associated with this "private diplomacy."

Several participants have mentioned to me the apparently limited number of persons that are authorized by the Soviet Union to participate in such conferences. As Ambassador Stoessel writes, "Representation on the Soviet panels dealing with U.S.-Soviet problems has tended to be heavily weighted in favor of the USSR Academy of Sciences' Institute of the USA and Canada." Still others, however, point out that while the discussions may begin with persons from this organization, once the importance of the participants and the seriousness of the discussion is apparent, the conversations often move to others, including those in official positions.

A second identified problem is that in some cases those on the American side approach the conversation either with inadequate preparation or with a certain naiveté about the possible effect of such discussions.

Landrum Bolling, who has long been involved in the Dartmouth Conference, pointed in a recent talk to several weaknesses or dangers involved for American interlocutors in these meetings. He cited amateurism, special biases, a limited understanding of foreign policy objectives, vulnerability to manipulation and disinformation, and the possibility that such conversations could delay or complicate official negotiations. Several have emphasized to me the need in such discussions for Americans to be well aware that the Soviets, whether ostensibly private or not, look upon these conversations as one more part of the long-term official dialogue.

Even on the American side these conversations are not totally free of government influence or totally invulnerable to the changes of mood in the basic relationship between the two nations. The U.S. government, like the Soviet government, has the capacity, if it wishes to do so, to suspend any conversations having any sort of official support.

Events that affect the overall relationship affect exchanges as well, as a portion of a letter from Senator Paul Simon illustrates:

> I was in Moscow in late December of 1982 and met with the Cultural Minister, as well as with other officials, and said we really ought to be getting cultural exchanges back on course. These had been largely discontinued by President Carter following the Afghanistan invasion. The response from Soviet officialdom was uniformly favorable, somewhat cautiously on the part of a few.
>
> When I got back, I met with Charles Wick, the head of USIA, and explained to him that I felt it was in everyone's best interest to further exchanges between the United States and the Soviet Union. We would better understand their system, and they would better understand our free system. Among other things, I felt and still believe that the ultimate impact of that is to open the door of freedom slightly in the Soviet Union.
>
> He called in perhaps 20 or 30 of the top people in USIA, and I spoke with them about it. Then I urged him to talk to President Reagan about it.... I received word that the President was favorably disposed to the idea, and negotiations then commenced.
>
> Exactly where we were in the negotiation process is not clear to me, but then the Korean airliner was shot down; and it was not only the passengers and the plane that were shot down, but the negotiations on the cultural exchanges.

These essays and comments also point to the difficulties in such conversations of obtaining insights into Soviet processes. While there can be extensive discussion of Soviet policies, there are few insights provided into the means by which such policies are developed, the relative relationships of institutions and personalities in the Soviet Union, and divisions that may exist within the Soviet councils regarding such issues as Afghanistan.

The Soviet participants in these conferences may, as they appear to many, be genuinely interested in a better understanding by each country of the problems of the other. There is no indication, however, that the presence of Soviets on these delegations suggest that they have either the position or influence to convey back views of the Americans that may run counter to Soviet policy or that might be likely to affect Soviet policies. The Soviets dealing with Americans may have a credibility problem with their own officials as may some Americans dealing with the Soviets.

Finally, on the Soviet side, while there may be nuances, it seems rare that there are any basic differences from official policy. I can recall some years ago hearing a presentation by two men each one of whom had been in the Soviet Union during the weeks before, one in an individual capacity as an editor and the other as part of a larger delegation. They gave presentations suggesting that they had gained special insights into Soviet thinking. At the end of the presentation, questions from the audience brought out quite clearly that the Soviets had avoided, with each, questions they did not wish to discuss and had said to each virtually the same thing.

Do these exchanges make a difference? Do they have an effect on official policy? Landrum Bolling points to one case in which the exchanges of the Dartmouth Conference might have played a role in a Soviet decision, namely in the U.S.-Soviet communiqué on the Middle East of October 1, 1977. Whether or not there was a direct link, it suggests that proposals made in the forums of private exchanges may lack the broader political perspective that can be expected of government. The communiqué, while it may have represented a positive step, was quickly denounced. It was not acceptable within the broad spectrum of American political life.

If there were no private exchanges with the Soviet Union, there would be strong efforts on both sides to develop such exchanges. Clearly they have a value in education and perhaps in providing human elements to the Soviet-American dialogue. There is little evidence that they have a major effect upon the making of policy on either side or in the resolution of the fundamental differences that exist between the two countries. Perhaps the value and the limitation are best summed up in the following paragraph from one participant:

> Who knows what one really learns during a visit to the Soviet Union. My Soviet hosts were invariably courteous, generally guarded, but sometimes offered me a flash of insight through comments, questions or disagreement among themselves. On such a visit, one feels that he is groping in a black box through a limited point of entry. But that is still more interesting than staring at it from a distance.

*****

Postscript. On December 9, 1986, as this book was about to go to press, one of its authors, the Honorable Walter J. Stoessel, Jr., died of leukemia in Washington, D.C. at the age of 66. A distinguished career Foreign Service officer and expert in Soviet affairs who served three times in Moscow, the last as U.S. ambassador in 1974-76, Ambassador Stoessel retired in 1982 after serving as deputy secretary of state. As a *Washington Post* editorial observed at the time of his death, Walter Stoessel was "the model of a professional diplomat [who] embodied the Foreign Service ideal. He served his government and his country well."

The Institute for the Study of Diplomacy dedicates this volume to the memory of this outstanding diplomatic practitioner.

Private Diplomacy
with the Soviet Union

1

Nonofficial Exchanges with the Soviet Union

Walter J. Stoessel, Jr.

T HERE ARE MANY VARIETIES of nonofficial exchanges between the United States and the Soviet Union. These include youth exchanges, contacts between "peace groups," and citizen exchanges, involving in some cases special target groups, such as, women, teachers, and doctors. Other, relatively structured, discussion groups concentrating on security, economic, and scientific/educational themes are organized by, among others, the United Nations Association's Parallel Studies Program with the USSR, the Dartmouth group, and the National Academy of Sciences.

During my three tours of duty in Moscow with the American embassy (the last, 1974–76, as ambassador), I was most familiar with the latter category of exchange groups, i.e., those focused on security, economic, and scientific/educational subjects. The embassy was usually advised well in advance of the plans of a given group to come to the Soviet Union, was occasionally involved in visa or other organizational problems connected with the visit, and was always pleased to arrange briefings for the group, if requested. The embassy, either at its own initiative or at the suggestion of the visiting group, frequently offered a dinner or reception for the group and its Soviet contacts. Depending on the nature and level of the group, such affairs were hosted by the ambassador himself or by senior embassy officers. These occasions offered the possibility of inviting Soviet representatives who were specialists in their fields and who were outside the restricted range of usual embassy contacts. From this standpoint alone, I found the visits of the various exchange groups to be useful to the embassy in broadening its knowledge of Soviet society.

As for the actual discussions held by the groups with their Soviet counterparts, the utility to the embassy varied widely. In some cases, an embassy officer was invited to sit in on the discussions as an observer (similar arrangements being made for a Soviet embassy observer when the group met in the United States). This was almost always useful to the embassy officer involved, often providing an opportunity for him to meet Soviet specialists he would not otherwise know and for expanding his knowledge of Soviet and U.S. views on the matters under discussion.

For the most part, the embassy did not participate directly in the talks of the various groups. Some briefed the embassy on the course of their discussions, while others did not. In general, the embassy found briefings of some utility. Although both Soviet and U.S. groups always made a point of emphasizing their nonofficial, nongovernmental status, the comments of Soviet participants usually confirmed well-known Soviet positions. On occasion, however, they provided nuances of interpretations or particular bits of information that were helpful in understanding Soviet policies or in forecasting potential changes in such policies.

Since retirement from the Foreign Service, I have become involved as a participant in nonofficial U.S.-Soviet exchanges in my capacity as chairman of the United Nations Association-USA Parallel Studies Program with the USSR. This program, funded largely by grants from public foundations, operates through two panels, one on security and one on economic subjects. Each panel meets with a Soviet counterpart panel on the average of once a year (although meetings have been held more frequently), alternating meeting sites between the Soviet Union and the United States. The UNA-USA panels are composed of private individuals with some degree of background and experience in the subject matter. As appropriate, experts are brought in for discussions of a particular topic.

Before each meeting with the Soviets, the UNA–USA panel arranges for briefings by U.S. government agencies on the official U.S. positions with regard to agenda items. Following the meeting with the Soviets, the panel is debriefed by government officials on the course of the talks. Through these procedures, the panel ensures that it goes into a meeting with the Soviets with a good understanding of the positions of the government, and the Soviet side knows that the U.S. panel speaks against this background, although always unofficially and with the clear understanding that the panel is made up of private individuals who can—and often do—express personal views at variance with those of the U.S. government. The briefing-debriefing arrangements also convey to the Soviets the seriousness of the U.S. side and the assurance that the views they express will be made known to the U.S. government at high levels.

I understand that other groups, such as the Dartmouth group and the National Academy of Sciences, follow more or less similar practices in order to ensure that they are well-prepared for the discussions with their Soviet counterparts.

On the Soviet side, the makeup of the panels is different. Given the nature of the Soviet system, it is inevitable that all participants have a kind of official status. Some, as in the case of representatives of various ministries or the Central Committee of the Communist Party, are officials on active duty. Others are from one or another officially sponsored institute or the Soviet Academy of Sciences. While all Soviet participants stress in discussions that they are speaking unofficially and informally, it is not to be expected that in their remarks in a full group meeting they will deviate from the basic, official Soviet "line" on the subject under consideration. It often is the case, however, that the emphasis and interpretation given to aspects of the Soviet official position may be of interest, and the atmospherics accompanying Soviet presentations are sometimes revealing. But the official themes are always present.

I have found, nevertheless, that the meetings can be quite

useful. A well-prepared U.S. group can, if it listens carefully, pick up in Soviet statements new points of emphasis or nuance that have not been previously expressed. At the same time, the U.S. participants, through their presentations and extemporaneous comments, can present American points of view that may be new to the other side and helpful to the Soviets in explaining the rationale behind U.S. thinking. The Soviet participants invariably pay close attention to U.S. statements and presumably report them back in detail to the Soviet party and government bureaucracy.

In addition to the discussions in the panels, there is of course a great deal of personal contact and exchange of views that takes place on the margin of the plenary group meetings. This type of encounter is often the most rewarding and beneficial for both sides. Its value is enhanced when, as is the case with the well-established exchange groups, many of the participants on both sides have developed good personal relationships over a long period of time and thus feel more at ease with each other.

One general problem affecting most exchange groups is the limited number of discussion partners available on the Soviet side. Representation on the Soviet panels dealing with U.S.-Soviet problems has tended to be heavily weighted in favor of the USSR Academy of Sciences' Institute of the USA and Canada,* with the same institute members meeting with a variety of U.S. groups. In addition, a few officials from the Ministry of Foreign Affairs, the Academy of Sciences, and several journalists seem to be "regulars" on the exchange group circuit and take part in many meetings with a variety of U.S. groups. Most of the latter have endeavoured to broaden the circle of Soviet representation, with some—still limited—success. The UNA–USA panel, for example, have recently met with representatives from the Central Committee and the Academy of Sciences who had not previously participated in exchange group discussions. It appears that there has also

---

*Other English-language versions of this institute's name abound—the Institute for the Study of the USA and Canada, the Institute for USA and Canada Studies, among others.—Ed.

been a reinvigoration of the Soviet UNA organization that may lead to some changes in the pattern of representation on the Soviet side for the UNA panels.

While I am not closely acquainted with the experiences of other, less formally organized, U.S. exchange groups, I have the impression that many of them have also encountered a similar problem of having to deal with a strictly limited number of contacts on the Soviet side. Also, I understand that those groups interested in promoting travel and reciprocal visits by U.S. and Soviet citizens to their respective countries have found that such travel is quite unbalanced in the sense that the flow is mainly to the USSR, with a relatively small number of Soviet citizens permitted to travel to the U.S.

In spite of these and other problems, my sense is that the nonofficial exchange groups play a useful role in enhancing communications between the United States and the Soviet Union. Official or nonofficial, these are difficult enough under any circumstances, and any additional lines of discussion that can be opened and maintained are to be welcomed. This is especially true during periods of heightened tension between the two countries, when official contacts tend to be constricted. Nonofficial exchange groups, by and large, continue to function at such times, even though the tone of the discussions often reflects the difficulties of the official relationship.

It behooves American nonofficial exchange groups to prepare for their sessions with Soviet representatives with care and thoroughness, and they must always be on guard against being used for purposes of Soviet propaganda. I believe experience has demonstrated that, if such guidelines are followed, nonofficial exchanges can play a positive role in overall U.S.-Soviet relations.

2

Informal Diplomacy: The Dartmouth Conference Experience

Philip D. Stewart

THE PRINCIPAL AXIS of conflict in the world today is Soviet-American relations. The emergence of over one hundred new nations since World War II, the rise of China and Japan as major powers, the sharpening of the North-South conflict in the mid–1970s, and the enduring Middle East crisis have all made challenging demands on the delicate fabric of the international system. Yet, the fact that only the Soviet Union and the United States have the capability utterly to destroy civilization as we know it continually forces questions of the management of U.S.-Soviet relations to the center of attention of governments and publics.

The central question of our international relations for almost forty years has been how to deal with the Soviet Union. For about fifteen years following World War II, these questions were deemed the exclusive prerogative of official diplomacy. This approach was reinforced by a broad bipartisan consensus behind the policy of "containment." Late in his administration, President Eisenhower recognized that the policy of containment alone was inadequate to prevent either the growth of Soviet global influence or major crises in U.S.-Soviet relations. The collapse of his efforts at building bridges through establishing a personal relationship with Khrushchev convinced Eisenhower of the limited utility of official diplomacy in breaking down the ideological barriers separating the two countries.

Reacting to these difficulties, Eisenhower urged Norman Cousins, then editor of the *Saturday Review,* to see if he could arrange a meeting between private American and Soviet citizens in the hope that citizens might be able to make progress where diplomacy had so far proved fruitless. After more than eighteen months of negotiations with the Soviet Peace Committee, a small group of Soviets journeyed to Dartmouth College in October 1960 to meet with a similar group of Americans.

While the talks during this first, week-long meeting addressed many issues, from the prevention of nuclear war to possible joint aid programs in the Third World, there were no significant substantive breakthroughs. What did occur, however, may have been more important. In the course of many hours of talks across the table, in the corridors, and along the pathways of the campus, distinguished and influential Americans and Soviets came to see each other as full-blooded human beings, with genuine attachments, beliefs, and ideas. The personal, human bonds growing out of this experience provided the essential foundation for the gradual development of the Dartmouth Conference into an informal communications channel through which the most complex and emotionally charged issues can be constructively addressed.

In the twenty-five years since this first gathering, the Dartmouth Conference has met in full plenary session approximately once every two years. Since 1981, smaller work groups, or task forces, on regional conflicts and on arms control have met at intervals of approximately six to eight months. While the Ford and Johnson foundations provided the funding for the first five sessions, since 1970 the Kettering Foundation of Dayton, Ohio, has assumed primary financial and administrative responsibility for this dialogue on the American side. In the Soviet Union, the Soviet Peace Committee bears formal responsibility for Soviet participation. In practice, however, the Institute of the USA and Canada and the Institute of Near and Middle East Studies of the USSR Academy of Sciences are our primary Soviet counterparts.

Some Results of Informal Diplomacy

What have the twenty-five years of unofficial policy dialogue in the Dartmouth Conference accomplished? Does this experience suggest that Eisenhower's hope that private citizens might help to enlarge the role of "reason" in the U.S.-Soviet relationship was justified? Or, are the differences that still so prominently divide us so immune to the efforts of private, or perhaps even official, diplomacy that even our best efforts can have little more than "cosmetic" or psychological benefits?

To answer the question of whether private diplomacy can "make a difference," we must begin with some clarity about what private diplomacy, in principle, can and cannot do. Private diplomacy cannot substitute for official diplomacy. Private citizens are forbidden by law to conduct negotiations. Moreover, private diplomats are always far less well-informed about specific issues on the intergovernmental agenda than their official counterparts. Solving specific international issues through negotiation and other means, whether it is a question of strategic arms treaties or of securing Soviet withdrawal from Afghanistan, is the task of governments.

Private diplomacy seems best suited to developing the preconditions for problem solving, that is, to creating a readiness on the part of governments to consider moving toward the resolution of an issue. In pursuit of this broad objective, private activities may range from establishing contacts with appropriate private persons on the other side, to developing a clear image of the interests and perceptions of one's counterparts on particular issues, to creating new pictures or concepts about how a question of mutual interest might be resolved. On those relatively rare occasions when policymakers are seeking alternative approaches, private diplomacy may have a modest impact on contemporary policy. Normally, however, the comparative advantage of private diplomacy in U.S.-Soviet relations lies in fostering imagination and speculation about our mutual longer-term interests and their implications for the development of policy.

Dartmouth Conference experience provides many illustrations of private diplomacy of varying effectiveness. The most severe test of the Dartmouth process occurred during the third conference held at Andover, Massachusetts, in October 1962. No sooner had the delegates assembled than President Kennedy appeared on national television to announce the unacceptability of Soviet missile emplacements in Cuba. The first question for both Soviet and American participants was whether it was appropriate for this meeting even to take place in the midst of a nuclear crisis. Hasty calls to each government established that officials on both sides supported the idea of private citizens thrashing out the immediate and underlying issues in this crisis. One result, at least, might be to help clarify the thinking on both sides and perhaps also, from the U.S. perspective, communicate the seriousness of U.S. intent to secure by any means the removal of Soviet missiles. In fact, the conferees established a useful channel between Moscow and Washington, mediated by Pope John XXIII, through which a number of useful messages were passed during the crisis.

More than twenty years after this experience, both Soviet and American participants in that meeting note the impact of those days in Andover on their sense of the potential of private diplomacy. While their impact on the Cuban missile crisis was clearly marginal, the experience of confronting an international crisis together led each to perceive the importance of having a forum where informed and influential private citizens can address, in a relatively nonconfrontational, non-polemical manner, even the most fundamental and sensitive issues and concerns of their nations. More broadly, the participants report that this experience created an abiding sense of a common responsibility to prevent our differences from leading to direct, armed conflict.

Building on the initiatives of the international scientific community, the Dartmouth Conferences from 1969 through 1971 brought together a number of Soviet and American environmental scientists in an attempt to develop a framework for cooperative research on global environmental issues.

Our Soviet colleagues informed us that these discussions helped place these questions on the Soviet political agenda, and thus helped prepare the way for the formal agreements on scientific cooperation signed at the May 1972 summit meeting.

During this same period, the question of renewing Soviet-American economic relations was explored in Dartmouth meetings between such leading figures as David Rockefeller and Dzherman Gvishiani, vice-chairman of the Soviet State Committee on Science and Technology. The ideas developed in these exchanges found official expression in the U.S.-Soviet trade agreement of October 1972.

Some of the most promising, yet ultimately futile, dialogue on economic relations took place in 1972 and 1974, on possible joint ventures in the Soviet Union and Soviet interest in joining the International Monetary Fund and adhering to the General Agreement on Tariffs and Trade. At the time, the Soviet government was anxious to encourage substantial American investment in Soviet projects. For their part, American firms were only interested if they could be assured of a continuing return on capital and if they could exercise some influence on the course of production. By 1974, informal discussions had led to a consensus that joint ventures were an appropriate vehicle for this, but Soviet laws prohibiting any private ownership of capital stood as a major obstacle. Nevertheless, Soviet participants insisted that the real issue was not one of "principle" but rather the instrumental question of means. In their view, leasing would probably become the appropriate vehicle for a major role for American and other foreign capital in Soviet development projects. When the Jackson-Vanik and Stevenson amendments made the trade agreement unacceptable to the Soviets, official Soviet interest, and even private flexibility on these issues, vanished.

During the first half of the seventies, Dartmouth Conference discussions had seen private Soviet attitudes toward international economic institutions move from hostility and denunciation to active exploration of the specific conditions for Soviet acceptance and involvement. The global inflation following OPEC's action on oil prices, together with the failure of the U.S.-Soviet trade agreement, brought about a reversion to the earlier position that the Soviet-dominated socialist international trading system was the wave of the future.

The Task Force Approach

Under the conditions of general deterioration in U.S.-Soviet relations following the failure of SALT II ratification and the Soviet invasion of Afghanistan, a more intensive dialogue began in the form of small task forces on regional conflict management and arms control. Rather than exploring specific policy options, these dialogues pursue two longer-term objectives: developing a clear sense of the assumptions, expectations, and interests underlying policies of each side, and exploring approaches and concepts that may offer some basis for an ultimately more stable, more secure relationship.

The task force on regional conflicts has held in-depth exchanges on Afghanistan, Iran, the Persian Gulf, the Arab-Israeli conflict, southern Africa, and Central and Latin America. Each side appears to have acquired a heightened awareness of the thinking underlying the other's behavior and policy in these areas. In addition, considerable common effort has gone into thinking through approaches, conditions, and incentives that might increase the opportunities for parallel or cooperative actions to reduce the level of conflict in these regions. On occasion, some of the signals or ideas arising from these discussions have found reflection in official policy.

Recent sessions of the arms control task force illustrate some of the possibilities, as well as some of the pitfalls, of dialogue in areas under official negotiation. In addition to exchanging views on the ideas and concepts underlying formal proposals, the sessions of this task force have emphasized the issues each side feels are most critical to progress in official negotiations. Thus, especially in recent years, the U.S. side has stressed the need for greater Soviet flexibility on verification and compliance issues. The Soviet side continually made clear its views on including British and French

missiles in any INF [intermediate-range nuclear forces] agreement. At this level, the dialogue may marginally influence the
course of negotiations, although there is little direct evidence
of this.

A longer-range, yet significant, issue for American participants has been the question of how to strengthen strategic
stability. In all earlier discussions, the Soviet participants
universally treated this as nothing more than a device to
induce the Soviets to reduce their heavy missiles. However, at
a task force meeting in 1983, in connection with a discussion
of the Scowcroft commission's proposal for a long-term transi-
tion to small, single-warhead missile forces, the Soviet side did
recognize that the question of strategic stability may be worth
considering in this context. There are now indications that
this concept may become the basis for an extended discussion
of the preconditions for a more stable strategic environment
and of possible steps that might lead toward this goal.

In March 1984, four months after the Soviet Union walked
out of the arms talks, the Dartmouth arms control task force
met in Moscow. The American participants had some hope
that they might help entice the Soviet side back to talks by
explaining the extent to which American proposals, never
fully presented in Geneva, met expressed Soviet concerns. At
the same time, as reported later in the press, an American
participant carried a personal message from President Reagan for delivery directly to Konstantin Chernenko, the new
Soviet leader. From the moment of our arrival at Sheremetyevo airport, it was obvious that the Soviets no longer
considered us to be "private diplomats" but, rather, surrogates
for the U.S. government. They thus mistakenly believed our
purpose was to attempt to engage them in "negotiations."
Having rejected any "return" to the former negotiations, the
Soviet side used this meeting to send the message to the U.S.
government that neither in the guise of private diplomacy nor
in any other form would the Soviet Union agree to restarting
START* and INF talks. The message was made crystal clear

---

*Strategic Arms Reduction Talks

by rejecting direct delivery of the president's message and by refusing to permit any substantive exchange on strategic or intermediate nuclear weapons. Needless to say, the American side left Moscow feeling frustrated and abused.

Even after the agreement to begin new negotiations, in December 1984, the Soviet participants regarded this meeting as having been of great importance. In their view, this dialogue had "convinced" the U.S. government that if there were to be negotiations, they would have to be within a new, different framework. From the point of view of the dialogue process, this episode illustrates one of the central dilemmas of private diplomacy. If one's objective is to influence policy, however indirectly, the "closer" the participants are to policymakers the greater the likelihood the dialogue will have an impact. Yet, if participants are perceived as "too close" to their governments, this may so constrain the discussion as to risk losing the openness, flexibility, and creativity that distinguish private diplomacy.

There is a fine line, however, between private diplomacy being "too close" or "too distant" with respect to government. There are times when being seen as having the full confidence of the government may create opportunities for significant influence by informal diplomats. In late November 1983, during a meeting of the Dartmouth Task Force on Regional Conflicts in Moscow, Soviet participants made it unmistakably clear that if American or Israeli warplanes attacked Soviet installations inside Syria, this would very probably lead to direct Soviet involvement in the larger struggle. According to later press reports, this message, when communicated to the U.S. administration together with other factors, helped lead to a decision to remove U.S. Marines from Lebanon. In general, informal diplomats need to be close enough to their governments to be "worth" taking seriously, and yet independent enough to think creatively.

FOCUSING SOVIET AWARENESS ON DOMESTIC CONSTRAINTS SHAPING U.S. POLICY. One of the seriously complicating elements in the U.S.-Soviet relationship since at least the late sixties has been the inability or unwillingness of Soviet policymakers to understand the ways in which U.S. public opinion shapes and limits the options available to any U.S. president, especially in the conduct of U.S.-Soviet relations. Soviet human rights violations and Soviet behavior in the Third World, from the Middle East to Angola and Afghanistan, have provided recurring cases in point. Since the first signs appeared of possible improvement in U.S.-Soviet relations in 1969, raising the awareness of our Soviet counterparts about the centrality of these issues within the American political process has been a major objective of the Dartmouth discussions.

The assumption underlying our approach has been that Soviet willingness to listen and capacity to comprehend the significance of these questions would be increased by hearing distinguished American citizens, known to be committed to improved relations, present calm, analytical statements on these issues. Thus, in 1972, several well-known congressmen spoke on the impact that Soviet emigration policy would have on the Congress' freedom to act with respect to most-favored-nation status. In December 1975, in July 1977, and in May 1980, in task force meetings and in plenary sessions, a number of Americans, well-known to the Soviets for their efforts at improving relations, voiced their concern about the increasingly negative impacts Soviet actions in Angola, Ethiopia, and Afghanistan had had, were having, and would have on bilateral relations because of the adverse reaction of public opinion. In recognition of the significant gaps and distortions in the Soviet understanding of the shape of American public opinion and its impact on the Reagan administration's hard line, in May 1984, one of the nation's leading students of the subject presented a concise overview to the participants at Dartmouth XIV.

Obviously, these efforts have had little effect on overt Soviet behavior. Yet, we must recognize that the Soviets perceive the issues of human rights and support for "national liberation movements" as of high political significance for themselves, but largely irrelevant to U.S.-Soviet relations. We should also accept that it is extraordinarily difficult for Soviets to grasp either the concept of an independent public opinion or of a government meaningfully limited by it. In the light of these realities some small signs of movement in Soviet thinking become more meaningful. As half-hearted and ultimately disappointing as it was, the Soviet policy permitting substantial Jewish emigration throughout the seventies was undoubtedly based on the reluctant conclusion that this was a necessary price to be paid to American public opinion in exchange for a substantial economic relationship and arms control agreements. Private diplomacy, through Dartmouth and other channels, was undoubtedly one factor in leading the Soviets to this conclusion.

Limitations and Lessons

One of the inevitable shortcomings of private diplomacy is that even though those involved in this activity may shift their views as a result of dialogue, there can be no assurance that these changed perceptions will "trickle up" to policymakers. This seems partially to explain the "failures" to communicate the impact of Third World events on the bilateral relationship. There is evidence to suggest that at least several relatively senior Soviet participants did come to recognize the negative effects on détente of Soviet behavior in the Third World. Thus, in 1981, following several frank exchanges on Afghanistan and its impact, an American participant privately expressed his personal frustration at what seemed the utter lack of actual communication on this issue. A Soviet colleague responded that it was very important to hear clear, analytical assessments of Soviet policy by respected and influential Americans, because almost the only way in which critical contributions could be made in the Soviet internal debates was by quoting such sources.

In a task force discussion in 1982, reflecting on lessons that must be taken into account if there were to be any prospects for a future détente, a Soviet participant put forth his own view. While he believed that events in the Third World "should" not have an effect, the empirical reality was that they did indeed contribute significantly to the erosion of détente as a result of their impact on U.S. public opinion. This fact must be taken into account in Soviet policy in the future, he argued. However, when this idea was later raised with Soviet officials, it was universally rejected.

The principal lesson to be drawn from these "failures" of communication is the recognition that private diplomacy must adopt a long-term perspective. Assumptions underlying policy, especially in a society lacking procedures for critical discussion of foreign policy, tend to change very slowly, yet occasional signs of readiness for change have appeared. Dialogue seems to be important in encouraging this process.

A second lesson suggests the value of attempting to draw into the process a broad circle of those close to the policy-making arena. This should enlarge the prospect that altered perceptions may have a more direct impact on policy. Of course, it is often the case that the views of those at this level are deeply held and very resistant to change.

The Conduct of Informal Diplomacy

What organizational forms and procedural norms does the Dartmouth Conference experience suggest are most helpful in facilitating private diplomacy? At the outset, it is clear that there are no universal formulas or guidelines which, if followed, can assure that any particular goal of private diplomacy will be met. What works in one set of circumstances or with respect to one question may prove fruitless at another time or on another issue. Nevertheless, there are some features of this process whose value becomes clear again and again.

Relations of respect based upon professionalism, expertise, and straightforward honesty are the essential foundation of policy dialogue. Mutual respect is what makes possible discussions that penetrate beneath the surface of official stance and superficial argumentation. In the Soviet-American context this characteristic acquires exceptional importance.

Soviet participants are constantly alert to the complications that can arise from excessive openness, from departing too far from accepted positions, so their natural tendency is to repeat safe views. These complications are twofold. On the one hand, if Americans were to report as "new Soviet policy" what were intended only as tentative explorations, this could give erroneous "signals" to the other side. On the other hand, if American participants were to publish such Soviet remarks, citing the speaker by name, at a minimum this could have a chilling effect on future discussions. In short, even for those Soviets with official sanction to engage in "dialogue" with Americans, serious, open discourse carries risks.

At the same time, the best Soviet participants, our experience has convinced us, are professionally and personally committed to finding workable means for solving international problems in ways that do not harm Soviet, American, or third-party interests. Without a willingness to listen carefully to "officially unacceptable" ideas, to look at one's own and others' positions and interests analytically and with a degree of openness, these Soviets recognize, genuine common ground cannot be found. While this approach has been taken at times in nearly every subject area, from the Middle East to economic relations to arms control, it is probably the exception rather than the norm. Where it does occur, respect for the integrity, competence, and fairness of their American colleagues, often built up over years of contact, appears to account best for this quality of dialogue.

THE STATURE OF PARTICIPANTS. Beyond a sense that their American counterparts will respect and reciprocate trust and openness, Soviets seem to be constantly concerned about whether a given American participant is "worth" listening to or conversing with seriously. There are many characteristics that may make particular Americans worthwhile in this sense. Our Soviet counterparts do have a professional and political interest in learning firsthand the views of significant political, economic, cultural, scientific, and academic leaders. Through such contacts, Soviet analysts hope to gain more precise understanding of currents and trends in the American political system.

Central to developing a sustained Soviet interest in policy

dialogue is the belief that the views of American participants, in some way, "count" in the American political process. The participation of former, or more occasionally future, high government officials, congressmen, leaders of industry and commerce, academic experts with political ties to present or future administrations, and representatives of significant cultural or social groups contributes in a cumulative manner to the Soviet sense of Dartmouth as a "worthwhile" policy dialogue. In particular, the participation of David Rockefeller, long regarded by many Soviets as the real power behind American "monopoly capitalism," has given this dialogue a special visibility on the Soviet side.

Parallel concerns about the extent to which our Soviet counterparts "count" in the Soviet political context have been evident on the American side as well. Indeed, involving Soviet participants who are roughly equal in professional and political status to American delegations is a precondition for involving and sustaining the interest of those the Soviets would find "worthwhile."

There are three realities that make this intrinsically difficult to achieve in the Soviet context. First, opportunities for Soviet citizens not holding high official position to influence policy, even indirectly, are extremely limited. There are no real equivalents to our former government officials, congressmen, politically influential academics or businessmen. Yet, to actively encourage Soviet political leaders to participate in the Dartmouth Conference almost surely would be to abandon the advantages of "private" diplomacy. Second, experience has increasingly made clear that there is indeed a very limited circle of Soviet citizens who have at least some potential for influencing policy, are professionally competent, and authorized to engage in dialogue with Americans. At best, we can seek to encourage involvement of a larger proportion of this limited group. Finally, one institution, Georgi Arbatov's Institute of the USA and Canada, located within the Soviet Academy of Sciences, has acquired a dominant voice in managing unofficial contacts by Soviets with Americans.

Even within these limitations, however, Soviet participation has generally been at an appropriate level and increasingly included participants from important political institutions, most of whom have been able to adapt to the norms of "private" citizens engaged in private diplomacy. Although each side has exclusive authority to select its own participants, the growing sense of Dartmouth as a useful policy dialogue has encouraged greater Soviet and American responsiveness to suggestions about the kinds of individuals who would be regarded as useful participants. In recent years, Soviet delegations have included the chairman of the State Bank, the vice-ministers of finance and agriculture, the deputy director of the Central Committee's International Information Department, officers from the Soviet general staff, heads of academy institutes, and prominent "political observers" who often serve as consultants to the Central Committee. At the conclusion of meetings in the Soviet Union, it is customary that task force chairmen meet with appropriate officials from the foreign ministry or Central Committee.

Formal positions notwithstanding, the question of the actual or potential policy influence of any Soviet involved in private diplomacy is not easily resolved. Critics often charge that groups such as Dartmouth really have little value because those with whom we meet supposedly carry little, if any, weight in policy circles. There are two sets of counterarguments that can be made.

First, the goal of private diplomacy is not to influence directly either Soviet or American policy. It is to learn about, and to help indirectly to shape, the images of the possible that our own and Soviet policymakers bring to bear on policy problems. Professional analysts, political commentators, and experts in each country are often the source of new ideas, changed images, altered approaches. Of course, this may be a relatively long and indirect process. By this logic, the "right" Soviets are involved in the Dartmouth process.

Second, while formal institutions doubtless shape the patterns of policy influence in Soviet society, relationships based on personal ties are alternate and significant sources of influence. The Soviet cochairman of Dartmouth (with Yuri Zhukov, a Pravda commentator) is academician Georgiy Arbatov, whose possible personal ties with the Politburo are most relevant here. At the symbolic level, Arbatov is clearly a prominent figure. He is the only director of a foreign affairs institute who is also a full member of the party Central Committee, a body comprising the top 330 of the Soviet political elite. During the early seventies, he was reported to be a major advisor to Brezhnev on U.S.-Soviet relations. His ties with Andropov went back to the early sixties, when he worked with Andropov as part of a group of consultants under Politburo member Otto Kusennin. After Andropov assumed power, there were indications that Arbatov often met with him privately, or in the company of Gromyko. Finally, shortly after Chernenko's selection as general secretary, Arbatov was shown in a Pravda photograph with Chernenko and Ponomarev, attending a meeting with leading West German Social Democrats. Participants in that meeting reported Arbatov speaking in an assertive manner, only moderately deferential to his political superiors.

In short, both sides in the Dartmouth process appear to find the quality and level of participation as it has developed in the mid-eighties—competent, politically engaged professionals—appropriate to the goals of private diplomacy.

THE PLENARY FORMAT. Creating a sense of "potential" value is only a first step, however. The natural tendency of busy people with many interests is to look upon events such as a Dartmouth meeting as little more than occasions to try to "sell" one's counterparts on a particular viewpoint, or to make a speech, listen for a few hours, and then go on to other things. This tendency, visible at times on both sides, is fostered by the "plenary" style of meeting. In a plenary meeting, from thirty to forty Soviet and American participants attempt to converse around a single table. This mode, which for years was favored by many Soviet participants and some Americans, encourages speechmaking and propaganda. For their part, nearly every Soviet participant feels obliged to make a statement, often lengthy. Even where a clearly defined agenda has been agreed upon beforehand, seldom does meaningful and in-depth interaction take place.

Plenary sessions are not always or necessarily of little value, however. In our experience, plenary sessions can be effective for two purposes. First, when there is a well-defined subject of interest to most participants, a well-prepared plenary can lead to important substantive contributions. Let me offer two examples. Since the general state of U.S.-Soviet relations and political and other trends inside both countries often influence what is possible in any particular policy arena, whether arms control or the Middle East, plenary sessions are often used to exchange views on these broad questions. To encourage thoughtful, analytic presentations and discussion, each side presents its view of trends and policies in the other's country. Soviet and American participants have found the exchanges developing from this approach sufficiently useful that it has become a feature of recent conferences.

Plenary sessions have also served as a useful forum to which task forces report the results of their deliberations. As task forces meet both during full conferences and in the interim, these plenary sessions help to provide a sense of coherence and integration to the process as a whole. While the normal procedure is for Soviet and American cochairmen to report individually to the plenary, occasionally task forces have developed sufficient consensus to have the report made by either a Soviet or an American on behalf of the entire group. Where difficult and sensitive issues have been addressed, as is usually the case, such a procedure signifies the high degree of mutual respect and rapport developed within the task force.

THE TASK FORCE. Even within the more intimate environment of the task force—small work groups composed of four to five participants on each side—effective discussion is not easily developed. Several factors have combined, however, to make this an increasingly useful format during the past four or five years. As early as 1972, at the Seventh Dartmouth Conference, work groups were used as the primary locus of substantive discussion. While these talks often led to policy-relevant proposals, the one-to-two-year intervals between meetings and the moderately high turnover in participants made it difficult to sustain substantive dialogue. Since 1981, however, task forces have met regularly, at roughly six-to-eight-month intervals. This greater frequency of interaction, together with a more stable core of participants, has made possible a sense of continuing dialogue.

The inclusion of participants on both sides who perceive this process as a useful means of pursuing their professional interests in contributing to the resolution of a range of international problems has resulted in greater intellectual "engagement" in the process. The small size of the task force and the frequency of interaction reinforce the sense that each participant's contribution is of value. More thorough preparation than previously, more effective follow-up, and the development of a longer-term perspective for the discussions themselves have been natural and positive consequences of this development. Substantively, these qualities, I believe, have made open, exploratory discussions more the norm, and have resulted in the more frequent elaboration of ideas and insights useful in the policy arena.

Preparatory activity on the American side is designed to meet four basic needs: elaborating the network of informed and interested persons involved in the dialogue process; developing possible new approaches or ideas for discussion; ensuring that participants have a clear and precise sense of relevant official thinking and policy; and deciding upon a strategy for the substantive discussions themselves. As a result of the process of "engagement" encouraged by the task force approach, much of this preparatory activity takes place in the normal, professional routine of the participants. U.S. members of some task forces, however, have found it useful to conduct an informal seminar with fifteen to twenty colleagues, from in and out of government, before and after task force meetings. The preliminary seminar is designed to elicit a variety of perspectives on the substantive issues to be addressed, and to develop possible useful approaches or ideas. At the follow-up seminar, insights and ideas from the dialogue are shared and discussed.

On occasion, it has been found useful to prepare informal papers, either before or after meetings. Following a task force meeting on regional conflicts in 1982, for example, both sides prepared and exchanged papers laying out their ideas on possible principles or incentives for minimizing superpower involvement in regional disputes. These papers then formed the basis for several succeeding meetings. As meetings have become more frequent, focused, and substantive, however, written papers have played a less important role.

OFFICIAL INPUT. Briefings by senior government officials prior to meetings long have been an important element of private diplomacy. Their primary purpose is to reduce the likelihood that incorrect signals may be given inadvertently to the other side. This is not to suggest that participants feel bound either to support or to defend official views. Rather, within Dartmouth it has become a norm of discourse to make certain that official views, together with justifications and explanations, are fairly presented, with explicit recognition that these are the views of our government. Beyond this point, individuals pursue whatever ideas or views may contribute to the dialogue. Follow-up briefings with officials are regularly conducted at the conclusion of conference activities. Our Soviet colleagues indicate that they follow similar preparatory and follow-up procedures.

RULES, FORMAL AND INFORMAL. No matter how thorough the preparation, or how collegial the relations between Soviet and American participants, creating and sustaining a level of discourse that replaces point-making and stand-taking with joint grappling with difficult and complex issues is an often elusive goal. An important facilitating factor has been the mutual development and support of norms of discourse that discourage the former and encourage the latter. Some norms are formal and articulated. Others have taken root through practice as both sides have found them useful.

There are three formal rules. (1) Even if discussion papers are prepared prior to a meeting, no papers are to be read before the group. (2) There are clear limits, which are moderately enforced, on the length of interventions. Opening remarks by cochairmen are limited to five minutes, while individual interjections for the duration of the session are limited to three minutes. (3) Normally, each side alternates in making presentations. This avoids the situation where one side might mount a verbal "barrage" against the other and encourages give-and-take exchanges.

One almost inevitable element of dialogue with Soviets is delivery of a litany of complaints about American policy and behavior. This routine nearly always must occur before a more analytic discussion becomes possible. One of the very salutary developments in the arms control task force is the recent custom of explicitly devoting the first hour or two of discussions to "mutual recriminations." This open recognition of the need that both sides feel, especially in difficult times, to air concerns and grievances has helped to make even this tension-inducing element of dialogue more collegial. If discussions should descend to recriminations at a later stage of the meeting, the air is often cleared by reminders that the period for such remarks has already passed.

Particularly on contentious issues, there is an almost irresistible temptation to engage in polemical argumentation, in accusations, or in simple debate. Where meetings have been substantively useful, it has been due in no small part to the fact that both sides have largely resisted these approaches. In recent years, the norm of analytical presentations and responses has become more generally observed. This has been a self-conscious effort on the part of American participants, and appears to be reciprocated by the Soviet cochairmen of the task forces and many of the continuing participants. It is doubtless the most important norm of discourse in Soviet-American dialogue.

An illustration may demonstrate the impact of this norm on the quality of discourse. The Soviets approached a recent task force meeting with the clear objective of persuading the American participants to support the Soviet call for a new international conference on the Middle East. The Soviets apparently believed that their willingness to consider some preliminary, preparatory activities would perhaps be sufficient to make their case persuasive to us. Instead of rejecting the Soviet position outright, the American participants undertook a detailed analysis of the problems such an approach would encounter, emphasizing particularly why we felt the preconditions for a successful negotiation did not exist. We outlined alternative steps that, by a different route, might lead to many of the substantive outcomes the Soviets claimed to desire. The Soviets were so committed to their policy, which had been announced in mid-1984 as an official Soviet proposal, that even an analytic discussion almost reached an impasse. It is perfectly clear, however, that a polemical or argumentative approach would have led to a totally unproductive exchange. By patient, analytic presentation of the issues and of alternative ideas and, crucially, because both sides evidently were interested in such a result, in the end some common ground was found.

Conclusions

Throughout this analysis, the importance of a long-term perspective, of relatively frequent interaction on a continuing set of themes, has been emphasized. Change of perspective, developing and accepting new ideas, elaborating common conceptions with respect either to issues of security and defense or to regional conflicts—both of which touch on our most vital national interests—will occur, if at all, over decades, rather than months or years. If private diplomacy is to make its contribution, adequate and reliable financial and organizational support is essential. Since in the United States this is a private activity, its initiation and continuation require private financing. The natural source of such support is private foundations.

For all of its twenty-five-year history, the Dartmouth Conference has been fortunate in having generous foundation support. For the first four meetings, the Ford Foundation provided all necessary financial support. The Johnson Foundation carried the principal burden for Dartmouth V and VI in the late sixties, with some help from the Kettering Foundation. Since 1972, the Kettering Foundation has been the principal financial supporter of this effort, contributing organizational and managerial support as well. The Rockefeller

Foundation has been an essential partner in this effort since 1979.

This is not to say, however, that support for this form of dialogue is assured for the future. There are two issues that continually surface in decisions by funders about whether to support private dialogue with the Soviet Union. The first is whether a private foundation should assume long-term responsibility for an ongoing project. Most funders operate under the principle that support should not be "permanent." A foundation may provide "start-up" costs for a potentially worthwhile activity, but sustaining funding is expected to come from other sources once the activity "proves" its worth. The Kettering Foundation has dealt with these issues largely by conceptualizing Dartmouth as a long-term experiment in developing methodologies of private diplomacy. Support for Dartmouth thus falls within the foundation's programmatic commitment to research on approaches to central political and societal problems.

Whether the results of private diplomacy justify the effort is the second issue continually facing potential funders. Here the central tension is between the natural desire for contemporary "evidence" of effectiveness and the subtle, incremental, usually difficult-to-discern yet potentially vital accumulation of changes in perceptions and images of the possible and desirable that arise from private diplomacy, but whose effects on policy and behavior may appear only in the future.

Though these questions are inherently difficult to answer, this analysis of twenty-five years of the Dartmouth experience does suggest that private diplomacy has made some modest progress toward eroding the ideological barriers dividing the United States and the Soviet Union. Indeed, it is possible to assert, with some assurance, that President Eisenhower's hopes for private diplomacy were justified. At the same time, we must recognize that we have only just begun.

3

The Dartmouth Conference and the Middle East

Harold H. Saunders

W HAT DOES nonofficial dialogue among U.S. and Soviet citizens contribute to peace between the two superpowers? What makes such dialogue effective? For over twenty years, the Dartmouth Conference has brought together influential citizens from both countries, alternately in the United States and in the Soviet Union. Since 1981, that process has been augmented by the creation of three small task forces to meet between plenary sessions. One has dealt with arms control issues. Another focuses on U.S.-Soviet relations in regions of potential conflict between them. Over the past decade, the Middle East has been a subject of particular concern. A third standing task force, on political relations, had its first meeting in January 1986 in Moscow.

What exactly do these groups and others like them accomplish? What can they not be expected to achieve? What are the dangers that nonofficial dialogue will undercut official policy? What makes them work?

An earlier version of this chapter was published under the title, "When Citizens Talk," in the *Kettering Review,* Summer 1984.

Dangers and Limits

First let's get the negatives out of the way. The most serious do not apply to the Dartmouth Conference.

During the twenty years I worked at policy levels of the U.S. government, in the White House and the State Department, our principal concern was that private spokesmen would somehow represent the United States in a way that did not accurately reflect either their authority to speak or the policies of our government.

Sometimes there is an almost deliberate misrepresentation of that authority, but more commonly there is simply the implication that individuals represent more than they do. Sometimes a consultant or person who has some contact with a senior policymaker drops the name and leaves the implication that he is accurately representing that policymaker's viewpoint. Sometimes there is a careless statement that "the White House thinks" a certain way about an issue.

On other occasions, members of Congress or private Americans have gone to another country and, in an honest effort to break an impasse at a time of crisis, have been tempted to promise more than they could deliver. For instance, during the hostage crisis, a member of Congress went to Tehran and discussed the possibility of congressional hearings as a way of meeting the Iranians' demand that their grievances be heard, only to find when he returned to Washington that congressional leadership rejected the idea. In other cases, individuals from the academic world have spoken with leaders in the Arab-Israeli-Palestinian conflict, suggesting approaches to solutions that their own government could not deliver.

These concerns can be quickly taken care of when both parties to the dialogue validate a particular channel. During the hostage crisis, for instance, two Paris-based lawyers became for a time intermediaries between the U.S. government and the authorities in Tehran because of their unusual contacts with Iranian revolutionary leaders. Their role was validated by an exchange of messages and tokens that made clear that responsible individuals on each side intended to work through that channel. Later, in the final stages of negotiating the hostages' release, the government of Algeria was affirmed as the acceptable intermediary by a formal exchange of messages. During the Cuban missile crisis, correspondent John Scali became a channel for a time when he was asked by a Soviet official to transmit an informal proposal to the U.S. government. Other examples will come to mind.

The Dartmouth Conference is clear on all counts. The exchange was initially arranged and has been continued with not only the full knowledge but also the encouragement of both the U.S. and Soviet governments. It is formally understood on both sides as a dialogue among private citizens, although individuals in both groups are known to have varying degrees of contact with their own governments. During the talks, a precise informal effort is made on both sides to understand as fully as possible who has what contact and influence with his or her government. Dartmouth succeeds in part because it involves individuals with policy experience and contacts, but remains nonofficial. Finally, conference leaders report fully to their governments. In short, the terms of reference are clear.

We have to acknowledge at the outset that such exchanges will rarely influence the next step in implementing an established policy course. Once a big government like ours has agonized through a difficult problem to a decision, it will not change course lightly. In truth, despite statements about the president really wanting to hear other points of view, the last thing a president sometimes wants once he has made a complicated decision is to have somebody give him another option. In the short term, government officials will listen to reports from the nonofficial dialogue, but will generally be swept along by the momentum of the present course of action. There have been exceptions, but it is not normally in that time frame that nonofficial dialogue is most likely to influence policy.

So much for the dangers and limits of such exchanges. What can they contribute?

"Ideas in the Air"

Turning to the positive potential of nonofficial discussions like the Dartmouth exchanges, we need to think for a moment about how policy is actually made to understand the points of entry for new ideas. I would zero in particularly on two points in the policy process.

First, there is a period early in any decision-making process when it is essential to define the problem facing the policy-makers. Sometimes, there are moments of redefinition as a problem drags on. That may sound like a sophomoric point but it is not. Often it is very difficult to place a problem into a conceptual framework. Even then, there will be heated controversy over defining the problem, because those who want to influence policy recognize that how a president defines a problem will initially shape how he decides to deal with it.

For instance, in 1978 there was an almost continuous debate over whether the Iranian revolution was made in Moscow or had been generated primarily from internal Iranian causes. As it happened, one picture of the problem included memory of a conversation in 1970 or so between an American professor and the Shah, in which the Shah had discussed how important it was to him to create political institutions that would keep pace with economic development. "If I can't solve that problem," he said, "my son will never rule Iran." That picture of Iran's struggle to maintain some parallelism between political institutions and economic and social change defined one way of setting the stage for dealing with the revolution. Others insisted that it was essentially a problem of public disorder encouraged by Moscow-supported groups and susceptible only of military resolution.

As another example, debate over the nature of the Palestinian problem has been heated. In some quarters, the Palestinians were first pictured not as a people at all and in later times only as "terrorists." Those holding such views deem any move to recognize equal Palestinian rights a threat to Israel's own identity, and they oppose such moves with all the vehemence they can muster. On the other hand, there are those who have accepted that the Palestinians are a people with rights comparable to those enjoyed by Israelis. Some recall that the United States in 1947 voted for a just partition of Palestine by creating both a Jewish state and a Palestinian Arab state. There are even those who probe the psychological needs of both the Israelis and the Palestinians and recognize the longing of each for acceptance by others, an idea termed "mutual recognition" in diplomatic parlance.

To repeat, how one defines the problem in debating it will begin to determine a course of policy. Such debate often continues for an extended period. Shifts in public opinion, meanwhile, provide a significant part of the environment in which policymakers view a problem, especially in the U.S. political system when administrations change.

The nonofficial dialogue with the Soviet Union over the years has increased understanding of the psychology of both peoples in dealing with the other and of real objectives on both sides. Private exchanges over the years have unquestionably introduced greater realism into the accurate definition of the problems of conducting U.S.-Soviet relations. Their first contribution has been to help put the problem in an accurate conceptual framework.

For instance, one definition of the problem of dealing with the Soviets in the Middle East is that they want to maintain "controlled tension" so they can spoil any effort to achieve greater stability by moving toward an Arab-Israeli settlement. The only policy prescription that can flow from this perception is one of confronting, blocking, and excluding the Soviets at every turn.

The quite plausible alternative picture that emerges from the Dartmouth talks—and from my last fifteen years of watching the Soviets at close hand in the Middle East—is that Soviet analysts do not believe a policy of "controlled tension" is realistic, because experience shows that no one controls mounting tension and that explosions produce Arab demands for military support the Soviets do not want to provide. The policy that would flow from judging that the Soviets may not be only spoilers is one of straightforward diplomatic discussion and analysis of Soviet actions to assess what measure of cooperation and competition is most likely to enhance stability—in both the Middle East and the U.S.-Soviet relationship.

Second, there comes a period in any policymaking process when options are considered and decisions made on a course of action. Often the most realistic definition of alternative approaches, especially when a government is already committed to one course, comes from political opponents or from neutral analysts outside government—or the government is forced at least to define its own options more carefully by policy debate generated in Congress or elsewhere in the larger body politic.

How are these views of the problem or alternative approaches injected into the decision-making process? As more and more of the participants in nonofficial dialogue, along with other analysts, write and speak of their views and experiences, certain ideas become increasingly current in the policy community, both in and out of government. Anyone who has participated in the policymaking process will affirm that the "ideas in the air" do influence the way public officials approach a problem, especially at the beginning of an administration when strong public opinion may press for new approaches, or when circumstances cause government to consider midcourse corrections in set policy, or when governments clearly hit an impasse. At those moments, new ideas find their way into policymakers' thinking. These "ideas in the air" often come first from the private sector, especially when they reflect changes in viewpoint. Here, it seems to me, is where the unofficial dialogue has its second opportunity for impact.

Participants in nonofficial dialogue have an opportunity, upon returning from their talks, to share alternative problem definitions and policy options with both policymakers and a wider audience. In the case of the Dartmouth Conference, the Kettering Foundation in 1983, through Washington symposia, redoubled its efforts to broaden involvement both in preparations for meetings with Soviet colleagues and in reports on the talks themselves. It has also attempted, through organizing meetings of all the American groups engaged in nonofficial dialogue, to increase communication among such groups to help sharpen their exchanges with Soviet counterparts, and to use these exchanges as a base for broadening the American people's understanding of the U.S.-Soviet relationship.

Laboratory for Learning: The Middle East Example

In this overall policymaking context, what kinds of specific contributions may stem from private dialogue?

First, such meetings can serve as laboratories for identifying the *human obstacles* to better official relationships.

In the Arab-Israeli arena, private meetings between Israelis and Palestinians have often been the only meetings possible, given the unwillingness of both parties to meet officially. Over the years, these meetings have been extremely productive in identifying what is necessary on each side to break through some of the psychological obstacles to official negotiations. Remember President Sadat's words to the Israeli Knesset when he visited Jerusalem in November 1977:

> [T]here remains another wall. This wall constitutes a psycho-logical barrier between us, a barrier of suspicion, a barrier of rejection; a barrier of fear, of deception, a barrier of hallu-cination without any action, deed or decision ... a barrier of distorted and eroded interpretation of every event and state-ment. It is this psychological barrier which I described in official statements as constituting seventy percent of the whole problem.

These psychological barriers can often be better understood in prolonged private dialogue than in official meetings with formal agendas.

Similarly, in the Dartmouth task force meetings, one factor in the U.S.-Soviet relationship comes through clearly. It is a strong desire of Soviet individuals to have their country seen as an equal participant on the world stage and not to be treated as inferiors. This comes through clearly in both official and nonofficial dialogue in Soviet bitterness over "exclusion" from the Arab-Israeli peace process since 1974. The thoughts behind the bitterness may be more fully expressed in non-official dialogue. To recognize this fact is not to urge that we drop our guard on any security front. It is to say that purposeful dialogue at an official level may require a more realistic "vocabulary" in recognizing what produces constructive Soviet responses. Some of that "vocabulary" may be more freely tested in nonofficial dialogue.

It has been particularly true in the period between 1981 and 1984, when the official Soviet-U.S. dialogue was at one of its low points, that private dialogue has provided insight into special Soviet concerns. Soviet responses to the administration's rhetoric about nuclear war, for instance, seemed far more genuine in face-to-face talks over a period of time than in official or quasi-official formal Soviet government retorts.

Similarly, when the overall Soviet-U.S. relationship became more businesslike in late 1984 and early 1985, the two governments seemed to see some value in talking about special problems like the Middle East in the context of the larger superpower relationship. Again, if they wished, they could consult the experience of Dartmouth participants who had engaged in such a discussion a few months earlier.

Second, private meetings can serve as laboratories for understanding or confirming *real interests* and how they are defined on each side.

Examples in the Dartmouth context alone are extensive. We have discussed at length U.S. and Soviet interests in the Middle East, the reasons for the Soviet invasion of Afghanistan, American concerns in Central America and the Caribbean, how our respective actions in Southern Africa have affected each other, and our concerns in Europe.

Specifically, when hostilities in Lebanon were at one of their peaks in late 1983, U.S. Marines were ashore, the guns and aircraft of the Sixth Fleet were offshore, and Soviet military personnel were manning the Syrian air defense system. At that time, a Dartmouth meeting provided the occasion for a precise statement of Soviet interests to be conveyed to Washington.

Similarly, but outside the Dartmouth Conference, since the United States government has prohibited itself from talking with members of the Palestine Liberation Organization, U.S. understanding of the thinking of PLO leaders has come from private Americans who maintain a dialogue with them, as well as from intelligence, from other Arabs, and from analysis of PLO actions. Insights into the interests of other such parties can also come from nonofficial discussions among Soviet and U.S. experts in the Dartmouth or other similar contexts.

Third, private meetings can serve as a place for identifying *alternative approaches* to an impasse that might meet needs on both sides.

Opportunities for this kind of refinement of approaches may be most common in the arms control area. The Dartmouth task force on arms control has this question on its agenda continuously. Regarding the Middle East, informal discussion before 1977 explored the conditions in which the Geneva Middle East Peace Conference might be resumed. The conference had met in December 1973 under U.N. auspices and Soviet-U.S. cochairmanship. When the new Carter administration took office and began immediately to discuss terms of reference with the Middle East parties, there was at least a background of informal dialogue with the Soviets on how negotiations might be resumed.

Fourth, private meetings can provide an opportunity for discussing and even testing *methods for improving machinery* to be used by the two governments in dealing with each other in a crisis.

The Dartmouth task force on U.S.-Soviet relationships in areas of potential conflict has attempted to develop a conceptual framework that would take into account (a) the 1972 Nixon-Brezhnev Declaration of Principles; (b) the task force's discussions of how each side defines its interests in the areas of potential conflict; and (c) recent work and discussion in Dartmouth and other nonofficial groups of principles of crisis avoidance and management. The Dartmouth task force tries to use its discussion of specific areas like the Middle East, Central America, and Southern Africa to advance its analytical framework for understanding Soviet-U.S. relationships in regions where conflict might provoke superpower confrontation.

The ideas developed in these groups may not necessarily show up quickly in policymaking circles. As I have said, governments are locked into their own tracks and can move from them only at certain points, as when a relatively new problem arises or an old track hits a dead end. What the nonofficial dialogue can offer is to alter perspectives and to define alternatives that have been tested in discussion for use at the moment in the policy process when change is required. This is not to say that these changed perspectives and possible alternatives cannot be produced by government. Secretaries Kissinger and Vance both maintained a direct informal dialogue with the Soviet ambassador in Washington. At Camp David, officials in all three parties conducted private as well as official exchanges. At some points, however, this may be better done through private channels. At moments in U.S.-Soviet relations when the official dialogue is strained or almost nonexistent, nonofficial exchanges may offer a more effective forum.

One other point needs to be made. Nonofficial dialogue is a vehicle for informing private citizens in each country. Often when our government seems to be floundering, it is an informed public that may create the environment and even the pressure for governmental decision. Our republic needs an informed public. Since the public does not participate in the exchanges between governments, it can be nourished through nonofficial exchanges.

In conclusion, the measurement for the success of nonofficial dialogue between nations is not immediate impact on policy. Its success lies in its contributing a sensitive picture of the problem to be faced and, as moments of impasse approach, alternative ways of approaching those problems. At those moments, it is the "ideas in the air" that, often as not, provide insight into new approaches. Those ideas can be developed, examined, and crystallized when citizens talk. The Dartmouth Conference exchanges provide one of the more successful examples of sustained nonofficial dialogue.

4

The Dartmouth Conference Process: Subjective Reflections

Landrum R. Bolling

AFTER A DECADE of involvement in Dartmouth Conferences and the subsidiary American-Soviet working groups, I still find it hard to define with precision and objectivity what we have accomplished and what we have learned. Again and again, at the end of our meetings, I have asked my American colleagues: "Was this really worthwhile?" On occasion I have put the same question to some of the Soviet participants and to U.S. government officials with whom we have discussed our experiences.

The answer, invariably, has been yes—even though at times a qualified yes. There is, of course, abundant good will on both sides for the idea that Soviet and American citizens should talk more with one another. Yet it is inevitable that the Americans, and almost certainly the Soviets as well, should question whether this particular type of structured discussion has genuine value for our respective interests and for improving Soviet-American relations. Neither side can find much satisfaction in any dialogue that gets lost in platitudes or in all-too-familiar political rhetoric. (In this aspect of Soviet-American competition we have surely reached strategic and tactical parity—in many venues!)

Beset as we are by mutual suspicion, apprehension, and substantial gaps in knowledge of one another, neither side wants to "give anything away" or to look foolish. The "safe" thing, therefore, is to do a lot of verbal sparring, with frequent resort to generalities and predictable political pronouncements representative of national and ideological biases. Dartmouth Conferences, especially in plenary sessions in the earlier years, experienced a fair amount of talk of this kind from both sides. Yet the pleasing fact is that as we have gained experience in the dialogue process, reached a certain level of personal acquaintance, and developed some measure of trust, the quality of our conversation has improved. Our dialogue has become more straightforward, relaxed, and good-humored.

Still, the question is: Are we accomplishing anything? What are the risks that what we are doing is either pointless or counterproductive?

In their independent, freewheeling approach to any topic, with no control and only minimal briefing from their own government, the American participants may unintentionally misinterpret U.S. positions, or so some people fear. We certainly give mixed signals from time to time—at least to any Soviet American-watcher who might be looking for an unambiguous monolithic U.S. "line." Conversely, how confident can we Americans be that we are getting a clear reading of Soviet policies, intentions, interests, and desires? Is there something significant lost in the translation, or in our understanding of what they say? To what extent may they be feeding us deliberate disinformation?

The Soviet participants are assumed to be under instructions; they are further assumed to be accompanied by one or more KGB agents in each delegation. (An inescapable guessing game among the Americans is trying to identify the KGB man.) Clearly, the Soviet delegates are under greater constraints and pressures than the Americans. At times, particularly in the opening plenary sessions, they have seemed programmed to record loyalty to some standard Soviet line on the topics at hand, with ritual denunciation of the United

States and defense of Soviet policy and action. Although this kind of communication is naturally off-putting to most Americans, it does have the merit of giving us direct from Soviet mouths an authoritative version of official Soviet policies and attitudes. Moreover, once these pronouncements are taken care of, we progress to a congenial and informal mode of dialogue. Discussions that start out stiff and stylized often turn into relatively free-flowing conversation. There is a general tacit agreement of sorts that there are limitations on candor that the Soviets will not cross—nor should we ask them to.

The American participants have no common party line to expound and defend—and would be unlikely to agree if one were required. Nonetheless, we sometimes do present the Soviets with a solid-front attack on their policies and a defense of ours. In such situations, it is not hard to imagine that the Soviet delegates jump to the conclusion that we have indeed had official instructions, after all. And one gets the impression that they would be pleased if they could be sure that were the case. They obviously want to be in touch with U.S. "ruling circles," and to be clear about their views.

The more our delegation seems to be plugged into our national establishment, the better the Soviets like it. They are delighted when we bring a retired U.S. military chief of staff or a former National Security Council director or a leading U.S. senator. Most of all, they appreciate the presence of David Rockefeller, a faithful long-time member of the Dartmouth team. Always the impeccably courteous gentleman, he is admired as a person and judged to be as near to the center of the American "ruling circles" as you can get.

We keep reminding our Soviet colleagues that we are a private, nonofficial group and that we speak our individual minds. Thanks to the Soviet political and social system, however, and the assorted roles their participants play within the system, they inevitably take on an unmistakable official coloration. Thus, there is a built-in asymmetry between the two groups from the start.

Moreover, there are long intervals between the full conferences—from a year to eighteen months—and there are usually several new faces at each meeting. Consequently, there is always a bit of a problem with getting reacquainted and integrating the newcomers into the dialogue. Finally, when our meetings end and we report to our respective governments, it is difficult to get any clear reading on what impact, if any, our discussions, observations, and interpretations may have on the thinking of those with official responsibilities.

Analyzing the Process

All this is by way of saying that we have problems when we are asked: "What specifically has the Dartmouth Conference accomplished in the quarter century of its existence?" With all the main negative or questioning judgments one may make about this endeavor, it has to be said, nonetheless, that it is a remarkable experiment in international communication. In the complex network of Soviet-American relations, official and nonofficial, the Dartmouth Conferences play a truly significant role; and we continue to readjust their format and reappraise their potential. If this kind of forum did not exist, we would be well advised to invent something like it.

One must keep in mind that the Dartmouth Conferences, even after twenty-five years, are still an experiment of sorts. There is an ad hoc quality to almost every meeting, and that feature has advantages as well as disadvantages. The agenda is almost never tightly structured; the daily schedule is subject to alteration by mutual agreement of the Soviet and American cochairmen. The emphasis given to a particular topic is likely to vary depending upon the level of expertise available and the depth of interest on one side or the other. Issues of importance to our governments are blended with concerns of the individual participants.

Part of our task is to interpret as clearly and honestly as we can what our governments' positions are and to analyze the consequences, actual and potential, of their differences. On the American side, we generally have seen these meetings also as opportunities to explore alternatives for change in those positions and in our countries' relations with each other. Understandably, the Soviet delegates are more inhibited about these explorations and almost totally resistant to any temptation they may have to imply criticism of anything their own government has done. Nonetheless, they show refreshing imagination at times in searching for new approaches to old problems, and they do not reject out of hand new ideas put forward by the Americans.

What is clearly satisfying to both of us is to reach, by whatever tortured route, a level of communication in which ideological differences have faded into the background and polemics have been put aside. Directness of dialogue, in which we can talk as rational human beings about actual problems in the real world, is appreciated by both sides.

The exchange of official notes, the conversations of ambassadors and foreign ministers, summit meetings of heads of state, and the signing of treaties—these are all important elements in the conduct of bilateral diplomacy. But they are facilitated or hindered by a thousand varieties of communication and by countless acts large and small that mold the perceptions of the American and Soviet peoples and their leaders, reinforcing their fears or encouraging their hopes. In the normal flow of events misperceptions are not uncommon. Attitudes and feelings of the people and leaders of one country toward another, toward its peoples and its policies, are shaped by what they think they know about the other—much of which is untrue or distorted—and by how they react to the overall atmospherics surrounding their relations.

This is not to suggest that all or most international disputes are based upon "misunderstandings" or irrational "emotions." Genuine conflicts of interest do exist and frequently occur. Nor is it sensible to suggest that they would be eliminated or prevented if there were just "better communications." Yet, surely, the broadening, deepening, and sharpening of our dialogue, at all levels, can contribute to a greater knowledge and sounder understanding, and to a general climate conducive to more responsible official decisions, policies, and actions.

There is no way to prove that these worthy objectives are

accomplished through the Dartmouth Conferences. There is no indication that the ups and downs of Soviet-American relations have been affected in any significant way by these meetings. They have certainly not prevented crises in our relationships such as arose in the wake of the Soviet invasion of Afghanistan or following the shooting down of the Korean airliner. Even when we have tried to warn our Soviet partners of serious consequences of a Soviet course of action, there is no indication that our advice ever reached the men in the Kremlin—or, if it did, that it made any difference.

During the seventies, at the time the Soviets were just beginning their interventionist policies in Africa—notably in Angola and Ethiopia, through their Cuban surrogates—American delegates at one of the Dartmouth Conferences protested vigorously and at length.

"Look," we said, "you keep declaring how devoted your government is to détente. You want us to negotiate arms agreements, expand Soviet-American trade, and do all kinds of other good things to promote a live-and-let-live accommodation. Yet, you have embarked on a kind of military adventurism that is guaranteed to outrage the U.S. government and the American people. You are undermining the good relationship with the United States that you claim is so important to you. Why?"

"You can't be serious," was their reply. "Angola is not important to either one of us. Differences of opinion between us over which political faction should control the government in Luanda surely can't be significant enough to affect the relations between the two superpowers. We both have too much at stake in maintaining a peaceful and balanced accommodation between our two countries. In an age of nuclear arms, it is the Soviet-American relationship that is of vital concern to both of us, not what happens in some small African country far removed from our borders. Only inflammatory propaganda aimed at creating anti-Soviet hatred and provoking conflict between our countries could build up tension over Angola."

"If that is what you believe," we responded, "you are deceiving yourselves. Anti-Soviet propaganda is not needed to sour our relationship. If you persist in these activities in Africa, ordinary Americans are going to see the Soviet Union as untrustworthy, insincere about détente, expansionist, aggressive. You may want to ignore it, but public opinion in the United States will increasingly turn against you. Just remember what we are telling you: the Soviet Union will pay a high price in terms of good will in the United States for what it is doing in Africa."

Five years later, with détente clearly falling apart, some of us who participated in that debate over Soviet policies in Africa reminded the Soviet delegation's old-timers of our earlier warning. They, of course, did not agree that we had been correct in our prediction—any more than they admitted mistakes about later, more sensational Soviet actions like the invasion of Afghanistan.

The Soviet representatives, in turn, like to remind us that the United States has not paid sufficient attention to Soviet suggestions for Middle East peace nor heeded their warnings about U.S. policies in the region. In our many discussions of Soviet-American relations in areas of regional conflict, focusing mainly on the Middle East, we have been exposed repeatedly to the Soviet analyses of the Arab-Israeli conflict. In detail, they have explained their perceptions of the deficiencies of U.S. policies in the region, the possibilities for peaceful settlement, and the right road to Soviet-American accommodation.

These are major points they have made at Dartmouth meetings, some as far back as 1974:

- Disengagement of forces (between the Israelis and the Egyptians and between the Israelis and the Syrians) that Kissinger is so proud of arranging is only a temporary solution; personal diplomacy cannot bring a permanent settlement. There must be an international conference to arrange a comprehensive agreement.
- The PLO has to be recognized as the legitimate representatives of the Palestinian people; you cannot have peace without taking their rights into account. The U.S. refusal to deal with the Palestinians is a mistake.

- You Americans are trying to exclude the Soviets from any role in making peace in the Middle East. You won't succeed. That region is in our backyard. What happens there is of vital interest to us. We have as much right as does the United States to be engaged in negotiating the crucial international decisions about that region. You can't make peace without us.
- You Americans, going back to Henry Kissinger and his step-by-step strategies, have tried to solve the Middle East problems piecemeal, playing off one nation against another, separating one issue from all the others. It won't work, and your government knows it won't work. Only some kind of comprehensive approach to a Middle East peace will succeed. The situation simply gets worse the longer the American approach is followed.
- The American government has such a pro-Israel bias, is so widely distrusted by the Arabs, that you have lost your credibility with them and cannot carry out your ambition to be the sole mediator. You need us as an active participant in peacemaking. You can't do it without us.
- Henry Kissinger originally worked out with the Soviet Union arrangements for an international conference on the Middle East to be held at Geneva under the cochairmanship of our two countries. It convened once and has never met since. A return to a Geneva-style international conference, which you once agreed to, is the only way out.
- Carter's Camp David settlement resulted in a separate peace between Egypt and Israel and nothing more, just as we warned. It deepened the split in the Arab world and opened the way for the Israeli invasion of Lebanon, which you Americans encouraged. That invasion was a disaster for the Lebanese, the Israelis, for everybody.
- We of the Soviet Union want to see peace in the Middle East. We could work together with you to bring peace. But that can happen only when you give up your determination to keep us out of the peace process and your absurd and unjust plan to give Israel dominance in the entire Middle East.

To this indictment of U.S. policies in the Middle East we have replied with citations of Soviet activities throughout that troubled region:

- The Soviet Union has again and again played a mischievous role in the Middle East. Repeatedly, you have sold arms and given encouragement to the most irresponsible, rejectionist elements in the region—Colonel Gadhafi, for example.
- You undertook, at one time, to make Egypt into a virtual Soviet satellite, with twenty thousand Soviet military and civilian advisers in that country. In addition to the massive arming of Libya and Egypt, you also poured weapons into Syria and Iraq—far more than could be justified by their defense needs.
- Since 1967, when you broke off diplomatic relations with Israel, you have refused to deal with one of the two principal sides in this conflict. How can you hope to play a peacemaking role until you recognize Israel?
- Despite your occasional words of opposition to terrorism, the Soviet Union has refused to use its influence with its client states, such as Libya and Syria, to persuade them to stop supporting the terrorist gangs that are a constantly disruptive element in the situation.
- Your repeated call for an international peace conference is misguided, premature, and unhelpful. It could have meaning only after careful, extensive preparation and quiet negotiation. Without that, a conference would be a waste of time, and a likely disaster.
- The Soviet Union has supported Arab positions, demands, arguments, and acts of violence so undeviatingly that it lacks all credibility as a mediator, or even as a critic of the American role.

How a totally objective outsider would rate our debates on the Middle East is problematic. However, it is clear that we have not convinced each other. Indeed, it is doubtful if scoring debaters' points in this way accomplishes very much toward advancing understanding, although there is a case to be made for blunt, honest, clear confrontation of our differences. Polite vagueness has little to recommend it. If there is to be any constructive outcome, it will emerge only after there has been a straightforward exchange on the substantive points at issue.

Exploring Alternatives—The Middle East

The basic challenge is to get beyond debate and explore the possibilities of agreement.

Any search for that constructive outcome involves risks. It presupposes the willingness to believe that, just maybe, some worthwhile measure of agreement might be reached. It also requires each side to lay aside its rhetoric, suspiciousness, and conventional "realism" and to imagine, perhaps, a theoretical solution to some problem on which we could agree. Occasionally, we have experienced such a daring adventure of the unfettered mind.

In December 1975, in a small suite in the St. Regis Hotel in New York, we held one of the first of a series of informal working party meetings devoted primarily to a single topic—in this case Middle East peace. On the American side were former Ambassador Charles Yost, Norman Cousins, and Landrum Bolling. On the Soviet side the participants were Vitali Zhurkin, vice-director of the Institute of the USA and Canada; Igor Belyaev, vice-director of the African Institute; and Alexander Kislov, a researcher in the U.S.A. Institute who had served as a foreign correspondent in the Arab world. All of us had had extensive experience in the Middle East, and a couple of us had just visited the region.

Even including support staff, we were a small group, comfortably fitting into a homelike setting. Making speeches at each other would have seemed wholly out of place. Moreover, we already had at least some acquaintance with each other. We quickly agreed that we would swap general overviews of the Middle East situation and of the elements of an Arab-Israeli settlement. While we did not agree on all points, or on the merits of our respective governments' policies toward the region, we found we had many common perceptions of the objective facts concerning the Middle East and its warring peoples.

We quickly established mutual respect for the firsthand knowledge each side brought to the discussion. We found we could agree on the gravity of the situation and on the fact that the interests of both the United States and the Soviet Union were threatened by a continuing failure to find an acceptable resolution. We agreed that the volatile forces at work in the Middle East could not be controlled by either of the super-powers, and that revolutionary developments could turn out to be both anti-American and anti-Soviet. (That was our judg-ment before the Ayatollah Khomeini proved the point, at least in Iran.)

We discovered we both seriously doubted whether a settle-ment was likely to be produced by the processes then being employed through the United Nations, or through unilateral actions by either the United States or the Soviet Union. We began to ask whether it was possible that the United States and the Soviet Union could agree on any new joint approach to the problem. Was it conceivable that, despite our great rivalry and mutual distrust, we could devise some new approach that would produce significant progress? We were not sure. We did believe that if our two governments could agree on an ap-proach to at least some of the issues in the Middle East, as we had done in the passage of UN Resolution 242 on November 22, 1967, following the war in June of that year, things might change for the better. On that cautious note, we decided to play a kind of "what-if" game. What if our two governments were to commission us to draft a resolution for the United Nations Security Council to consider—an updating of UN 242, jointly sponsored by the USA and the USSR?

We started with what our governments had already agreed to, the principles laid down in UN 242. We went on to acknowledge that its provisions had not been implemented and that the issue of the rights of the Palestinian people, beyond their needs as "refugees," had not been addressed. What proposal on this question, if any, could our two nations jointly support? It was a daunting task. We argued over every phrase. We debated at length over the meaning of individual words. But, in the end, we arrived at a statement that all six of us agreed ought to be forwarded to the responsible officials in our governments. Our "draft resolution" affirmed explicitly the right of Israel to exist as an independent sovereign state, behind secure and agreed boundaries, and the right of the Arab Palestinians to govern themselves under some form of self-determination. It seemed to all of us a reasonable and modest enough proposal. We went back to Washington and Moscow and passed it on to our governments. Silence. We do not know what our Soviet partners heard; we Americans heard nothing.

Half a year later, Dartmouth X convened in the desert resort of Rio Rica, in southern Arizona. Our working party on the Middle East, slightly changed in membership, picked up where it had left off in December. Our discussions were brisk and limited, but reaffirmed the positions we had agreed upon in New York. Specifically, we called for "joint or parallel" action by the two Great Powers to bring about a general peace in the Middle East, recognizing the national rights of both the Israelis and the Palestinian Arabs.

More than a year elapsed before Dartmouth XI met, in July 1977, in the Baltic seaside resort of Jurmala, in Soviet Latvia. There our American Middle East working party group included Joseph Sisco, former under secretary of state, who had been on the Middle East negotiating shuttles with Henry Kissinger, and lawyer Rita Hauser, a prominent New York Jewish leader and one of the authors of the Brookings Report on a Middle East settlement.

The Soviet delegation expressed strong disapproval of the new administration in Washington and charged that Carter's human rights campaign was a cover for trying to restart the Cold War. Despite the harsh Soviet tone in the beginning, we settled down to one of the most far-reaching, in-depth discussions of Middle East problems—and of Soviet and American relations to them—that we have ever had. Once again, it was agreed that both Great Powers should jointly affirm their support for "just and fair principles" for a Middle East peace, should endeavor to reconvene an international conference as rapidly as adequate preparations could be made, and should declare their commitment to protecting the rights of both the Israelis and the Palestinian Arabs.

When we left that Dartmouth meeting in mid-July, none of us, so far as I know, had any inkling that Foreign Minister Andrei Gromyko and Secretary of State Cyrus Vance were going to issue a joint Soviet-American declaration on Middle East peace, as they did on 1 October of that year. It caught the governments of Israel and the Arab states by surprise and touched off an immediate angry debate in many capitals. Israel denounced it out of hand. So did Syria. Yasir Arafat endorsed it at once. Meanwhile, the Israeli government mobilized its supporters in the United States to bring pressure on the White House and the Congress to repudiate this statement of belief and intent—it was hardly more than that—and within five days it was a dead letter.

Members of the Soviet Dartmouth Middle East working party look back on the Gromyko-Vance statement as the high watermark in Soviet-American cooperation on Middle East peace, and claim to see a direct link between it and the various Dartmouth Conference discussions we had had, going back to our attempt to draft a joint UN resolution at the St. Regis Hotel in 1975. Who knows? Neither Mr. Gromyko nor Mr. Vance ever breathed any suggestion of that to us. And since it was one of the swiftest failures in the long, tortuous course of failed Middle East initiatives, who can want to rush forward to claim any of the credit!

What should be said in summary, however, is that in the course of exploring exhaustively, over several years, the assorted viewpoints and interests of the Soviet Union and the United States with respect to the problems of the Middle East, we found much that the two countries had in common. We became convinced that each has an important stake in getting this conflict settled and a comprehensive peace established. We saw no likelihood that either power could any longer profit by continuation of a no peace/no war situation, and nothing but much human suffering and great danger for everybody in further warfare.

We found Soviet experts on the region talking in much the same terms about the objective facts and issues as their peers in the United States and moderates in Israel and the Arabs states. In our efforts to frame rational theoretical solutions, we were not very far apart. Indeed, Soviet-American cooperation on Middle East peace is a genuine possibility, at such time that both sides decide to pursue it in a sustained way. I believe that is the conclusion of both American and Soviet delegations to the Dartmouth Conferences. If we are correct, surely in time that possibility can be realized—before, we must hope, another Arab-Israeli war blows the area apart.

Lessons from Dartmouth: One Man's View

Spread over an entire decade for this participant, the Dartmouth Conference experience has taught me much: about the Russians, about the workings of their political system, about the processes of diplomacy, about the problems of communication, about the humanness of all human beings, about the limitations of power and the power of ideas, about the weakness of belligerence and the strength of kindness, about the widespread weariness with suspicion and the hunger for trust, about the fear of war and the hope for peace. In no particular order, let me set down some of those lessons—very personal lessons of one aging student who has learned a lot, remains uncertain about much of what he thinks he has learned, and is eager to learn more.

□ Diplomats have a tough job. They need to know a great many facts about the issues with which they are dealing and the partners with whom they are negotiating. And they will never know enough, nor ever be wholly certain about all the facts they think they have learned. They have to do a massive amount of homework and keep at it all the time.

□ There are severe limitations within which diplomats must operate. They must work within a given political system, under a particular set of bureaucratic guidelines, serving a defined policy identified with a government in power. They must carry out instructions whether they agree with them or not. They must defend their government's behavior whether they approve of it or not. They must be forever careful about what they say and what they do not say, and with whom they do and do not talk.

□ Those who are privileged to take part in nonofficial international communication—private diplomacy, it is sometimes pretentiously called—must, or should, operate under certain constraints as well. Unless they are directly commissioned to deliver official messages, and this sometimes happens, they must make it clear, again and again, that they are speaking as private individuals, not as spokesmen for the government.

□ Honesty with civility should be the watchword for the type of international dialogue we are examining. Real differences of viewpoint, of interest, of policy, should not be glossed over. Any meaningful understanding has to be based on a candid assessment of reality. Fawning words of concession and pretended agreement do not win respect or confidence. At the same time, it is important to state differences with dispassion and to listen attentively to contrary views, no matter how outrageous.

□ With nonofficial communicators as with official diplomats, there is no substitute for knowing what you are talking about. One cannot be overprepared. Homework on each topic to be discussed is essential.

□ Do not talk too much. Long-windedness is a bore in any language. Listen carefully, make notes of what is said, and make notes of what you want to say later. The most crucial part of the discussion is likely to occur after everybody has spoken once.

□ Keep a sense of humor. Grimness rarely wins the argument. A light touch at the right time is a great relief in tense discussions. A wit that recognizes the humanness of all is always welcome—well, almost always.

□ Big meetings, plenary sessions, are inevitable in all conferences, but the most productive talk is likely to take place in small informal groups. Big meetings, inescapably, call forth the actor, the polemicist in almost everybody who gets the microphone; this is true in every culture. Posturing, performing, making speeches at one another are forms of communication, to be sure, but not the most serious and productive means of deliberation.

 □ Listening is one of the most important skills, and one of the most neglected, among communicators and conference attenders. On the most elementary level, it is essential to stay alert and know what is going on. Misunderstandings based upon inattention not only break the rhythm of a dialogue but tend to weaken the credibility of the participant. Moreover, to develop the most constructive tone within a meeting, to have any hope of progress toward understanding and agreement, it is essential to give to each one who speaks the sense that he is heard.

The underlying purpose of the dialogue, in most cases, is to reach understanding, to eliminate areas of ignorance, to overcome stereotypes, to establish a process of ongoing communication—ideally, ultimately, perhaps to reach agreement. This is not easily or casually done. It cannot be achieved by wishful or sentimental thinking or pretty words. For there to be any hope for progress toward that goal it is necessary that a person be open and forthcoming, and that involves risks. Such a person makes himself vulnerable. But life is full of risks, and we are all vulnerable. We simply have to be awake and alert and to know what we are doing. And that isn't easy, either.

5

Private Diplomacy at the Highest Levels

Armand Hammer

I N THE SHORT SPACE of a fortnight in June 1985 I traversed the globe to have private meetings with three leaders who control our planet's destiny—Ronald Reagan, Mikhail Gorbachev, and Deng Xiaoping.

We talked business, of course—at the Kremlin and the Great Hall of the People we discussed the status of our joint ventures. At the White House, the business was to report to my own president on the remarkable progress being made in the national cancer research program in my capacity as chairman of President Reagan's Cancer Panel.

But, in each case, we also talked politics—world politics— and what could be done to lessen the threat of nuclear war and help bring the East and West closer together. I carried with me no diplomatic portfolio, but I did come well prepared, armed with a lifelong conviction that so-called private diplomacy can make a difference and contribute to better understanding.

It has been my firm belief that peace, stability, and prosperity in the world are not necessarily created by the men in striped pants so much as they are promoted by day-to-day contacts and commerce among the peoples and institutions of nations through trade that is fair and profitable to both sides.

We businessmen must leave to the statesmen the enormous

and delicate tasks related to the art of diplomatic give-and-take in the international arena. But in our own way, when the opportunity arises, we can make positive contributions to the process through our established bonds of mutual interest, just as long as these efforts do not infringe on sensitive negotiations related to national policy issues.

I was born shortly before the dawn of this century (four score and seven years ago, as a matter of fact) and I have seen too much war and misery to just stand by and do nothing. As I have throughout the years, I will continue to devote my energies to doing what I can to work toward a meaningful peace, whenever the occasion is appropriate to do so.

I'm known as the man with the "Russian connection" and more lately as a holder of a "China card." I see no mystique in these labels, although one is sometimes inferred (particularly by my competitors and those who think me too soft on communism—really socialism). I tell the Soviet leaders I'm a capitalist. I do not see socialism working. Perhaps the only country which has been successful is Hungary, where Kadar has mixed it with a certain amount of free enterprise or capitalization. When I told this to Kadar, he replied, "Not capitalism—human nature." While we differ in ideology, I see no reason why we have to destroy or threaten each other with nuclear destruction. We can engage in mutually beneficial trade, cultural and scientific exchanges, and let history decide which system is best.

After more than a half-century of involvement in East-West trade, I have learned that the best way for a chief executive to conduct business is at the top, especially as far as foreign governments are concerned. Bureaucracy is everywhere, most notably in the socialist countries, and you'd be quite surprised how much of the Red "red tape" can be swept aside if you conduct your business with the right people at the top of the pyramid.

My company, Occidental Petroleum Corporation, does business in fifty different countries on six continents, in places as diverse as the Soviet Union, Libya, the United Kingdom, Romania, Oman, Colombia, France, Pakistan, Italy, Peru and the People's Republic of China. I have made it a point to meet as many of the national leaders as is practicable.

In addition to the leaders of the Communist world, this has also brought me into personal contact with Prime Minister Thatcher, Presidents Mitterrand, Zia, and Pertini, King Fahd, the Sultan of Oman, and Presidents Betancúr of Colombia, Alfonsín of Argentina and Belaunde of Peru, to name a few.

Everywhere I go I find that solid business practices transcend ideology, if you are willing to work at it.

When I'm negotiating overseas, I wear two hats, as it were. Under one of the hats I am the board chairman of a major corporation, an ardent capitalist who has the responsibility to some 40,000 employees and 305,000 common shareholders to make the very best business deals I can negotiate. Under the other hat, I am a man who can look back over a lifetime of involvement in world affairs, who sees the possibility that a private citizen, acting on his own, can contribute to world stability by paving the way with good business intentions.

I have personally known every leader of the Soviet Union, except Stalin, whom I never had any desire to meet. Although I did not have a private audience with Mr. Andropov, an appointment for our meeting was on his calendar when he died. I guess I was closest to Leonid Brezhnev during most of the eighteen years he was in power, and we had six private sessions on some critical international issues before his death in 1982.

By the same token, I have known every U.S. president since Hoover and have had the honor of serving six of them in official and unofficial capacities over the years—Franklin Roosevelt, Harry Truman, John Kennedy, Richard Nixon, Jimmy Carter and Ronald Reagan.

My so-called "Russian connection" actually spans sixty-four years—from Vladimir Ilyich Lenin in the early twenties to Mikhail Gorbachev today—and it all came about by chance.

I first arrived in Moscow in 1921 as a young physician eager to help fight a terrible typhus epidemic that had broken out in the aftermath of the Revolution. I had just received my medical degree from Columbia College of Physicians and Surgeons and had six months to wait before starting a residency at Bellevue Hospital in New York City.

I guess I had a flair for business even back then. While I was a pre-med student, my father suffered a heart attack and asked me to take over his struggling pharmaceutical concern, which was on the verge of insolvency because of a dishonest business partner. I became a businessman most of the day and a student most of the night and was able to turn the company into a million-dollar success by the time I earned my M.D. My father had been a steel mill worker in his youth and joined the Socialist Labor Party. Later he was a leading member of the American Communist Party. My brothers Harry and Victor and I never agreed with my father's ideology. We were American first and last. At my father's urging, we sold about $150,000 worth of pharmaceutical and other goods to Ludwig Martens, the unrecognized Soviet ambassador, who was later deported.

I was one of the first Americans to come to Russia in the aftermath of the Revolution. Besides my interest in combating the typhus outbreak, I wanted to collect the money due our company. Not many individuals were granted visas in those bleak days, so to help assure entry, I purchased an old World War I mobile field hospital in France as a gift to the Soviet government.

I wound up stranded in Moscow in a miserable hotel, walking a bureaucratic treadmill as I waited to get to work. I was frustrated after several weeks and was just about ready to give up, when I was invited to join a group about to be sent to the Urals, where my hospital would be located. It was the most traumatic experience of my life.

The Revolution had wrought havoc; almost everything had been destroyed or stood idle. As we passed through the Volga District we saw thousands upon thousands of people fleeing without food. Trainloads of people were arriving at each station, and as each train arrived the dead would be carried out. Starving children and their parents pressed pathetic faces against the windows of the train, begging for a crust of bread.

The suffering that I saw on that trip is something I hope

never to see again. The real problem was famine and pestilence, not a typhus epidemic as I had been led to believe.

As best I can reconstruct that conversation of so long ago, I asked the local commissar how much grain would be needed to carry the people through the next harvest. "A million bushels", he replied.

"Well, I have a million dollars," I said. "There is a glut of wheat in the United States and the farmers are selling it for a dollar a bushel. I'll buy a million bushels and have it sent to you on credit."

In return, the Russians agreed to supply an equal amount of furs, platinum, emeralds and mineral products that I could send to the United States by return ship. The deal was completed, and the Russians threw in a ton of caviar for good measure.

A few days later I found myself in a tiny railroad station listening incredulously to a Morse Code exchange between our tour director, Mr. Martens, and Moscow. The man who had changed much of the history of the world, Vladimir Ilyich Lenin, wanted to see me at the Kremlin.

When we met, Lenin did not sound like the ruthless Red Tyrant he was portrayed to be in the West. Tears welled in his eyes when I told him of horrible conditions I had seen in the Urals. At one point he picked up a copy of *Scientific American* from his desk, thumbed through it, and said:

> Look here, this is what you people have done. This is what progress means ... buildings, inventions, machines, development of mechanical aids to human hands. Russia today is like your country was during the pioneer stage. Dr. Hammer, we don't need more doctors. We need business people who can get things done. The U.S. and Russia are complementary. We have enormous undeveloped resources. The U.S. can find here raw materials and the market for machines. Russia needs American techniques and methods. We are moving toward a New Economic Plan that will open trade with the West. Why don't you become the first foreign concessionaire?

That was the end of my promising medical career.

I remained in the Soviet Union for nine years, and during

the first part of that time, most of the trade between the U.S.S.R. and the United States went through my hands. I became the sole representative in Russia for thirty-eight American companies whose products ranged from tractors to fountain pens.

The first, and by far the toughest to bring in line, was the Ford Motor Company, then dominated by its cantankerous founder. Henry Ford was perhaps the foremost anti-Bolshevik in the United States in 1921. I made the long trip from Moscow to Dearborn and somehow persuaded him that communism was going to be around for a long time in the Soviet Union, so there was no sense waiting for a change in the government as he had hoped. I also told him that the Soviet people he scorned rated him on a par with Thomas Edison as one of the great living Americans, and that they would pay fully for every tractor he chose to send them. Mr. Ford agreed to do business. Later I was instrumental in getting the Fords to build the first automobile factory in Russia, on the banks of the Karma River.

After Stalin took power, however, the Soviet economic system underwent a radical change. Stalin decided he could build Russia without NEP and foreign concessions, relying on repressive measures and fear. The Russians instituted their own official trading company, AMTORG, and took over most of my concession operations.

In return, I was informed I could have any internal concession I wished, and I told them I wanted to build a pencil factory. They couldn't understand why until I told them that Russian pencils were so crude they tore the paper when you wrote and that good pencils imported from Germany cost the equivalent of fifty cents, far beyond the means of most Russians.

"You say you want to teach the people to read and write, and you don't have any decent pencils," I said.

I was granted the license and immediately set off to Germany to hire the experts from Farber to run the plant. I introduced piecework—a touch of capitalism in the citadel of communism. Within a year we were producing $2.5 million worth of pencils and doubled this a year later, even exporting them to such countries as England, China, Turkey and Persia. The plant, now known as the Sacco-Vanzetti Pencil Factory, still stands today on the outskirts of Moscow.

In 1930, I sold out all my interests in the U.S.S.R. Lenin, my benefactor, had died and I knew I could not do business with Stalin. I moved to France in a banking venture and then back to the United States, where my interests turned progressively to art, the distillery business, cattle breeding and finally to the most challenging and enterprising business of all—oil and related energy products.

Thirty years were to pass before I was to resume my "Russian connection." Several years before his election to the nation's highest office, I had been introduced to John F. Kennedy by our mutual friend, then Congressman Jimmy Roosevelt. I was impressed by this dynamic young man from Boston and strongly supported him when he was elected president in 1960.

Two days after the inauguration, at the suggestion of Senator Albert Gore, Sr., of Tennessee, Mr. Kennedy appointed me as a roving economic emissary, without portfolio, to help improve our trade relations across the world. Secretary of Commerce Luther Hodges arranged an extensive itinerary that would take me to the United Kingdom, France, West Germany, Italy, Libya, the Soviet Union, India and Japan.

The first part of the trip went according to form until I arrived in Moscow. As it turned out, the Moscow stop was so productive that I was ordered to cancel the remaining legs of the trip and return immediately to Washington.

After a polite meeting with two Soviet trade bureaucrats that went nowhere, I decided to take the bull by the horns and asked for an appointment with Anastas Mikoyan, the deputy prime minister. We had met three decades before in Rostov. Mikoyan was the local district commissar when we delivered the first Fordson tractors to Russia.

An embassy aide, laughing nervously, told me there was no way a deputy prime minister would meet an American capitalist businessman, but I insisted that a note be sent to Mikoyan anyway. Within two hours a car was dispatched to take me to Mikoyan's office.

I had a delightful meeting with this dour-faced old Bolshevik. We talked about the old days and shared a laugh when I reminded him of how some of the Rostov peasants fled to the hills when Fordson tractors arrived in town, mistaking them for enemy tanks. Then we settled into a serious discussion of Lend-Lease debts, credits, and increases in tourism and cultural exchanges.

The next morning, as I was about to leave for New Delhi, I received an urgent call from our embassy informing me that Nikita Khrushchev would like to see me at the Kremlin the next day.

We spent two hours in an exhilarating exchange in the company of my old friend, Anatoliy Dobrynin, who at the time was chief of the American Countries Division of the Ministry of Foreign Affairs. I had met Khrushchev once before, during his trip to California in 1959, and I must say at times during our discussions he lived up to his shoe-banging, "we-will-bury-you" image, boasting about great Soviet achievements in steel production, missiles, science and space, and condemning the U-2 incident that had occurred under Eisenhower.

He insisted that the Soviet Union should be treated by the United States on the same level as Britain and other favored nations. "If you give us credit, you should do so because it is to your benefit and not as a favor," he added proudly. He expressed a high regard for President Kennedy and described Mr. Eisenhower as a "noble and dedicated man who sincerely wanted peace . . . but he delegated too much authority and was lazy."

I repeated the proposals I had made to Mikoyan covering cultural exchanges and suggested the feasibility of a fertilizer exchange agreement. Khrushchev promised to consider my proposals and then proceeded to lecture me as follows: "If we cannot give our people the food, shelter and cultural benefits that you provide under the capitalist system, then communism is bound to fail. However, we are convinced that we can, and our performance over recent years is proof of this."

As I was taking my leave, I asked the Soviet leader if there was any message I could take back to President Kennedy.

"Yes," Khrushchev replied, "Tell him to lift the ban on Russian crabmeat."

I had been briefed on this seemingly inconsequential matter and explained that the official U.S. position was that the ban was imposed in the belief that slave labor was employed.

Khrushchev fumed with anger. "There is no slave labor any more in Russia," he said. "Not since Stalin died. They've been disbanded."

I suggested that they allow us to send in an inspection team to verify this, and then there would be no problem. Khrushchev would have none of it, reflecting the historic Russian passion for secrecy that goes all the way back to czarist times and has been a major stumbling block in strategic arms negotiations. Finally, he said he would be happy for me to go and see for myself, and I replied that I did not have the time.

As I departed he presented me with his personal automatic pencil topped by a ruby red star, in appreciation for the visit and for my establishing the first pencil factory in Russia. He also made arrangements for me to visit my old pencil factory before I returned home.

President Kennedy lifted the crabmeat ban shortly after I came back to Washington and reported to him. As it turned out, our intelligence people knew from the Japanese that there was no slave labor used in the Kamchatka crab-packing industry.

My high hopes for increased trade and warmer relations with the Soviets came crashing down a few months later, as a result of the abortive Bay of Pigs invasion. This was further compounded by the Cuban missile crisis in 1962 and Khrushchev's fall from power two years thereafter. My bid for a fertilizer deal wound up on the shelf after Khrushchev lost his job, but the seeds had been planted.

I had made two more trips to Moscow before Khrushchev was deposed and accomplished some breakthroughs despite the icy relations that existed during the sixties. The catalyst was one Mme. Yakaterina Furtseva, the newly named minister of culture and the first woman to reach such a high post in the Soviet hierarchy. We became fast friends right from the start.

During the course of our first conversation, Mme. Furtseva mentioned she had just returned from Copenhagen where she had been enchanted by an exhibition of Grandma Moses' bright primitive paintings.

I then made her an offer she could not refuse. I would arrange for Grandma Moses to come to the Pushkin Museum in Moscow if she in turn would send a collection of one of Russia's finest contemporary artists to the United States. And so it was done, in the midst of one of the most critical periods in U.S.-U.S.S.R.relations. Babushka Moses, as she was known, came to Moscow and, with the permission of the State Department, the works of a brilliant Russian icon painter named Pavel Korin were shown in the Hammer Galleries in New York. The press in both cities acclaimed the exhibitions a great success, devoid of propaganda.

To me it was a way of keeping some lines of communication open when the doors were closed.

Our paths crossed again in 1971 when Mme. Furtseva made a tour of the United States. We arranged for my own collection of "Five Centuries of Masterpieces" to be exhibited in the great museums of the Soviet Union in return for a U.S. tour of forty-one magnificent Impressionist and Post-Impressionist paintings, treasures that went back to the times of the czars and had never left the country before. They had been seen at the Hermitage and Pushkin by only a handful of American art critics, and the art world in general only knew of them through photographs.

The exhibition made a triumphal tour that included the National Gallery in Washington, Knoedlers in New York, the Los Angeles County Museum, the Kimball Museum in Fort Worth and, in response to a last minute appeal from Henry Ford II and Richard Gerstenberg, chairman of General Motors, the Detroit Institute of Art.

Other major art exchanges were to follow in the seventies, with the crowning achievement the showing of the Hermitage's masterpiece, the *Benois Madonna* by Leonardo Da Vinci, in museums across the United States in 1979.

I returned the favor last year when I brought the Codex

Hammer, the last Leonardo notebook remaining in private hands, to the Pushkin, where it was enthusiastically received.

Although I'm known as a medical doctor who practices business, I must confess that the arts are my true avocation. Throughout my life I have held the firm belief that the arts are one of the best means of establishing mutual bonds of understanding and friendship among the peoples of the world. Art is an emissary that transcends the boundaries of nationalism, race and creed, because it has a universal appeal.

I was to return to Moscow again, just two months after President Nixon opened the door to a new, regrettably short-lived era that we called détente, when he met Mr. Brezhnev at the summit in April 1972. I had received a message from Dr. Jerman Gvishiani, President Kosygin's son-in-law, to meet him in Paris. We had dinner and from that came an invitation to return to Moscow.

Times had changed. This time I was allowed to fly into Sheremetyevo Airport in my own corporate jet. I was well received. My past ties with the Soviet Union, my ability to speak Russian and, most importantly, my unique association with Lenin all worked to my special advantage. None of the members of the new regime had ever known or met Lenin.

Most of my meetings that week in July of 1972 were with Dr. Gvishiani, who was deputy chairman of the State Committee for Science and Technology. As I recall, it was brutally hot in Moscow and there was no air conditioning. We were attempting to put together a trade protocol, a framework for doing business between a sovereign state and a private enterprise—something that had never been done in the Soviet Union.

As many businessmen have found to their dismay in dealing with the Soviets, the negotiations did not go swiftly. In the hope of speeding up matters, I informed Dr. Gvishiani that we planned to depart from Moscow by dusk on the following day.

By midafternoon of the next day he called me to his office and presented me with a proposed protocol written in Russian Cyrillic. He suggested that I have it translated, studied, and then returned to Moscow in a month or so for resumed negotiations. No business deal with the Russians can be launched without a signed protocol. It provides the base from which all the details of the deal are initiated.

I found a way to circumvent the accustomed delays in reaching agreement. I read it through quickly, but carefully. I picked up a pen and struck out the work "draft" from the proposed agreement Dr. Gvishiani put before me.

"Occidental accepts," I told him.

Dr. Gvishiani was stunned. "Don't you want to study it longer and show it to your lawyer?"

"No," I replied. "It's something we can work under. It's your draft, not mine. I haven't changed a word, so why don't you sign it?"

He left the room to confer with his associates for a time, returned smiling and signed.

The Russians drive a hard bargain, and almost a year of intense negotiations followed before the ensuing contracts were signed. I made twenty-one trips to Moscow between July 1972 and January 1975.

Out of those trips came contracts to build a world trade center on the banks of the Moscow River, including a hotel, apartments and an office building for Western businessmen, and a unique twenty-year, multibillion-dollar fertilizer exchange agreement, which required the approval of President Nixon and the U.S. Congress. The trade center, known popularly as the Hammer House, was completed ahead of schedule and within projected costs. The fertilizer deal is now in its sixth year and continues to thrive to the satisfaction of both sides. It is a barter arrangement, the basic form of trade, in which Occidental ships as much as a million tons of super-phosphoric acid—called SPA—per year to the Soviets, in return for ammonia, urea and potash of equal value.

In contracts, the Russians are as good as their word and proved it when they continued to deliver their products to us, even when our shipments were banned by the 1979 embargo imposed by President Carter in retaliation for the invasion of Afghanistan.

Although I did not know Leonid Brezhnev at the start of our negotiations, we soon became good friends and remained so until his passing in 1982. He first called me to the Kremlin in February 1973 to thank me for sending him two original letters written by Lenin that had been in private hands up to that time. Unlike the somewhat austere Lenin and the sometimes pompous Khrushchev, Brezhnev was a bear of a man with a warm heart and keen insight who made you feel right at home. I often had to remind myself that within the Soviet sphere of influence, this was the man who ruled with an iron hand in concert with his chosen Old Guard members of the Presidium. We met again privately at Blair House four months later when Brezhnev made his own goodwill visit to the United States.

Over the next few years I was called upon on various occasions to relay some messages back and forth between Presidents Nixon and Brezhnev, and sometimes made overtures on my own. The topics included discussions of some of the Jewish emigration cases of that era, as well as means of improving trade and cultural relations.

In May of 1978 I was invited to the Kremlin again to receive the Medal of Friendship among Peoples, one of the highest honors that can be bestowed by the Russians on a foreign noncommunist, in recognition of "many years of activity aimed at strengthening mutual understanding between the United States and the Soviet Union." I had some other business to conduct as well.

A story making world headlines concerned Francis Crawford, an American businessman stationed in Moscow, who had been arrested by the Russians on charges of black market currency violations. The indications were the Soviets planned to make a "cause célèbre" of the case, holding an open trial with a stiff eight-year prison sentence in the offing. Before I left for Moscow, President Carter asked that I personally intervene to see what could be done.

Following the Kremlin ceremony, I flew to the Crimea, where a meeting had been prearranged at Mr. Brezhnev's summer retreat. He was supposedly seriously ill at the time, but he certainly didn't show it. He was out swimming off the beach in the Black Sea when I arrived.

We discussed the Crawford incident at length, and I expressed President Carter's serious concerns. Mr. Brezhnev showed me the evidence compiled against the man, even though Crawford expressed his innocence throughout the ordeal. We then discussed pros and cons of Crawford's fate, and what it would mean to deteriorating U.S.-U.S.S.R. relations if the Soviets decided to make an example of him.

I must say that in all my dealings with Brezhnev, he always displayed an even temper, was a patient listener, and was quick to grasp the nuances of the issue at hand. Above all, he was a pragmatist with the courage to make decisions.

As the affair turned out, Crawford was found guilty in a public trial that was covered by the Western press, but was given probation with orders to leave the Soviet Union.

I supported President Carter the first time he ran, and from the time he assumed office I urged him to meet with my old friend Brezhnev—the sooner the better. I have been a long-time advocate of summitry and remain so today. I feel it is vital that the leaders of the two superpowers get to know each other personally, and I have proposed that regular summits be scheduled every eighteen months or so, no matter who is in power.

I felt if these two men had met at the height of their powers, as was the case with Nixon in 1972, with détente still a reality, the situation might have been different. But by the time Carter and Brezhnev finally met in Vienna in June 1979, it was too late. Brezhnev was sick and aging. Carter's power was waning. The SALT II Treaty they negotiated was a good one, but it could not be ratified, even by a Senate controlled by Carter's own party.

Six months later, the ball game was over, as they say, when the Russians invaded Afghanistan. President Carter expressed to me privately after he left office that one of his great regrets was that the summit meeting had not taken place earlier in his term.

I met twice more with my old friend Brezhnev, in October 1980 and December 1981, mainly to try to keep the lines of communication open after the Afghan disaster.

In the October meeting, a tired and ailing Brezhnev, a

shadow of the vigorous "bear" I once knew, expressed surprise about the Western outrage against the Soviet intervention. As far as he was concerned the Soviets were reacting to a real threat that a government hostile to their interests could take control of Afghanistan on their southern border. The Russians have a phobia about their southern boundaries, believing they are flanked by hostile countries to the east (China) and to the west (Pakistan, supported by the U.S.). As far as Brezhnev was concerned, there was no alternative but to intervene, a course I'm sure the Soviets have come to regret.

Brezhnev told me that the Soviets would be willing to withdraw if the United States would guarantee noninterference and assurance that a hostile regime would not be set up in Afghanistan. I consulted with another friend, President Zia ul-Haq of Pakistan, and he offered to help solve this riddle. But President Carter and his advisors, absorbed as they were in a losing reelection campaign and the Iranian hostage crisis, were not ready to listen.

As we entered the present decade, I stated publicly that except for the Cuban missile crisis, our relations with the Soviets were the worst I had seen in the sixty-odd years I had been doing business with them. At this writing we have passed the Geneva Summit of November 1985 and anticipate the projected follow-up meetings. It is my earnest hope that we've come full circle again. I came away from my meetings with Secretary Gorbachev and President Reagan highly impressed and imbued with new optimism. The conditions for the Geneva summit were ideal. The timing could not have been better. And we have in Ronald Reagan and Mikhail Gorbachev two charismatic and popular leaders who have expressed the sincerity and goodwill to accomplish high purposes.

To show his flexibility, Mr. Gorbachev told me as I was leaving his office, "I know America can live without Russia. And I know that Russia can live without America. But this is not good for either country or the rest of the world who look to us for stability and world peace."

For his part, President Reagan has been calling for a new

beginning in U.S.-Soviet relations ever since his historic speech of January 16, 1984. As he said at the time and has reiterated often since: "Together we can strengthen peace, reduce the level of arms, and know in doing so that we have helped fulfill the hopes and dreams of those we represent and, indeed, of people everywhere. Let us begin now."

My readings of history have convinced me that wars begin when communications break down. As for myself, I plan to keep on trying, for where there is communication there can be understanding, and where there is understanding there can be reason. Understanding and reason are the hallmarks of a meaningful peace.

I'm mindful of the words of the late Lord Philip Noel-Baker, a Nobel Peace Prize winner with whom I was associated for a number of years in the cause of peace and human rights. Lord Noel-Baker, who dedicated a lifetime to this noble endeavor and who died a few years ago at the age of 93, was often asked why he continued to work so fervently and speak out so eloquently for a purpose that seemed so futile in the face of history.

"I am often discouraged, but I become more resolute to go on," he replied. "All the heritage of the extraordinary genius of the human race is at risk."

I believe there is a lesson there for all of us.

Armand Hammer's "private diplomacy" has not always been with the Soviets. He was involved, as a private citizen, during World War II in assisting in the famous destroyers-for-Britain effort. He has written this vignette of the relationship with Franklin and Eleanor Roosevelt that grew out of that role as a private citizen.

One foray into world affairs came at the outset of World War II when I worked with President Roosevelt and Harry Hopkins in developing the destroyers-for-bases proposal with Great Britain. I was and am today a great admirer of Roosevelt and had supported him in his first two terms. Senators William King of Utah and Henry Hollis of New Hampshire recommended to the president that I serve as a consultant on various plans to help Great Britain during the pre–Pearl Harbor days.

It was the time of the Hitler-Stalin pact, which I vehemently denounced, and I set to work at the president's request to help sell the proposal to swap fifty mothballed U.S. destroyers with Britain in return for U.S. use of a number of their military bases in the Western Hemisphere. The job was much tougher than it sounds today when you consider the isolationist fervor that had gripped much of the country and the Congress prior to our entry into the war. Britain desperately needed the destroyers to help combat the German U-boats in the North Atlantic that were devastating the convoy supply lines, and we needed the use of the bases as stepping stones for our aircraft and navy in event of war.

We launched a massive 'P.R.' campaign through the use of pamphlets and telegrams to influential Americans and news editors to put the program over the top—and the strategy paid off. It was an early milestone in the eventual Allied victory.

I'll never forget the first time I came to call on President Roosevelt at the White House, and the memory comes back to me on every succeeding visit I have made there. When I arrived I was ushered into the office of "Pa" Watson, the president's appointments secretary, only to be informed that the president was tied up in a meeting. After sitting patiently for a half-hour or so, I was joined by William C. Bullitt, the first U.S. ambassador to the Soviet Union, whose appointment was to follow mine.

While we were chatting I took note of a pair of over-sized dice on Watson's mantle. Watson explained that they were the gift of General G.W. Goethals, of Panama Canal fame, and that the dice were in fact carved from some lumber used in the canal construction.

One word led to another until Watson proposed, "Let's have a crap game while we wait." The three of us squatted on the floor, Indian-style, pulled out our wallets and proceeded to roll.

Another half-hour passed before the president's meeting ended. When Watson brought me into the Oval office to present me to FDR he said, "Mr. President, you should listen to this man. He's very lucky. While we were waiting for you he took $600 from Bullitt and me shooting craps!"

I had the opportunity to get to know Roosevelt and Eleanor better as the war years went by. FDR was a unique combination of steel and empathy, and he had great warmth and a keen sense of humor.

Out of respect for the Roosevelts, I later purchased their Campobello Island summer retreat, which had fallen into disrepair, and restored it to its original state. During the last year of her life, Eleanor Roosevelt spent the summer with me and my family. She wrote my brother Victor shortly before her death:

> On this my last day at Campobello, I want to thank you again for your great kindness in letting me stay in the cottage and for arranging everything for my comfort. I have had a most delightful time, topped off today with one of the most beautiful days the Island could produce and ending in a glorious sunset.
>
> I am leaving much, much stronger than I came and I attribute the renewal of my strength to the peace and quiet I have found here.
>
> Words cannot express my gratitude to you and Irene but I do hope you realize that it is deep and warm.
>
> Looking forward to seeing you both very soon, and hoping you will come to visit at Hyde Park before long.
>
> Affectionately, Eleanor Roosevelt

Less than a year later, I donated the compound to the governments of the United States and Canada to be administered jointly as an International Peace Park.

6

Business Negotiations with the Soviet Union

Robert D. Schmidt

R EPEATED ENCOUNTERS with various Soviet agencies and officials in my capacity as vice president of Control Data Corporation have required the full use of practical techniques of salesmanship, persuasion, and negotiating tactics developed over thirty-five years in business.

One learns in that sensitive society to observe "symmetry of position" in dealing with Soviet counterparts and to avoid negative, threatening words in favor of softer and—to them—more acceptable language. The Soviets never seem fully to understand the difference between official and private individuals and are continually looking to businessmen like myself to provide clues to U.S. policy or to influence such policy. Other concepts, such as the joint venture, seem just not to be transferable between our societies. The differences mean that one must be constantly alert to avoid legitimate misunderstandings. In dealing with the Soviet Union, one is not in downtown Des Moines, Iowa.

The Soviets proved to be sensitive, also, over any suggestion that they were receiving outdated, "used" or inferior equipment. They wanted the latest. As the complexity of equipment and the problems of the security of technology grew, this meant that the U.S. businessman was constantly in the middle between U.S. and Soviet authorities. The businessman could, at the same time, detect within the U.S. government the tug-of-war between those who saw business opportunities as a way to improve relations and access to the Soviets and those who saw sales as a threat to our security.

Dealing with the Soviets and the United States in the business world is a constant learning experience.

*   *   *   *

Control Data's initial contacts and business negotiations with the Soviets started in the late 1960s and were encouraged and supported by the U.S. Atomic Energy Commission. At that time, through the efforts of a staff member in its West German subsidiary, the company contacted computer science representatives in the "science city" of Dubna in the USSR and secured an order for a used computer. Thereafter, I personally made a trip to the Soviet Union to meet with the head of foreign relations for the State Committee of Science and Technology (GKNT), who was responsible for the contacts between the computer business in the Soviet Union and foreign businesses such as Control Data and IBM.

My initial meeting with the representative of GKNT was a somewhat grim experience. He let me know immediately that he considered Control Data a neophyte in the computer business and hardly a match for the very credible reputation of the IBM Corporation. "From where did you get the audacity to believe that you could provide computing equipment or computing cooperation with such an important country as the Soviet Union when we already have such a wonderful company as IBM?" was the way he put it. After he had gone on in this vein for almost thirty minutes, I lost my temper and stopped him. I apologized for disagreeing with him, especially in such a blunt fashion, but said that his knowledge of the computing industry in the United States and other parts of the world was sorely lacking. To relate the wonderful IBM company and its computers to the important country of the Soviet Union was at best a non sequitur. I told him Control Data had a reputation for producing the world's largest and fastest scientific computers and had attained that reputation with the design and production of the CDC 1604A,[1] of which Dubna was now one of the proud owners. Although I was not in the Soviet Union at the time that initial computer order had been placed, I believed it was important for me to be there to carry on the negotiations for its delivery and installation. I described to him in some detail the capabilities of not only the CDC 1604A computer, but also the new CDC 6600, which was being sold throughout the industry and the world.

I could not tell whether he was deliberately provoking me or whether he was one of those people who use a provocative attitude as a ploy to gather more information by putting one in the position of defending one's product or service. In retrospect, it did not matter, since I achieved my objective of getting Control Data included in future competition for computer systems in the Soviet Union.

As a result of these preliminary contacts and direct negotiations, Control Data obtained the order in early 1968 for the used CDC 1604A, which was already out of production in the United States. It was to be installed at Dubna at the Joint Institute of Nuclear Research (JINR), an open research institute that produces data used by scientists the world over.

With the official encouragement of the U.S. Atomic Energy Commission, it took a very short time to get an export license. Later, however, when an order was placed by Dubna for a new CDC 3600 computer, a machine of more than three times the power of the CDC 1604A, the export license application did not receive such expeditious treatment.

This second export license was obtained only after a series of negotiations Control Data conducted with JINR scientific and administrative people, the Ministry of Foreign Trade of the USSR, the U.S. Department of Commerce and the U.S. Department of State. Also, new requirements were placed on Control Data by the Department of Commerce to secure an end-use guarantee from the Soviets that the computer would be used only at Dubna and only for research for peaceful uses of atomic energy, and to ensure U.S. entree to the computer

---

[1]An appendix at the end of this chapter provides data on the equipment discussed by the author.—Ed.

site at any time. The Soviets were somewhat reluctant to guarantee that access could be provided at the site at any time, mainly because of the visa requirement for travel from Moscow to Dubna, a distance of ninety kilometers. Several trips to the Soviet Union were required to discuss the form of the end-use statement and the guarantees. At length, all parties became satisfied with the terms of the agreement and the export license was approved.

This sale was followed by another sale some years later of a new machine, initially the CDC 6400, on the order of three times more powerful than the CDC 3600, but then upgraded in the course of our discussion to a CDC 6500.[2] Control Data's application for an export license for the 6500 was again supported by the Atomic Energy Commission, because at that time Dubna had the world's largest linear nuclear accelerator and the United States was interested in the data produced there.

The licensing negotiations with the Department of Commerce and the Department of State followed the pattern of the previous discussions on the CDC 3600, but with some strengthening in the language and in the guarantees required by the United States. This necessitated more discussions with the Soviets over how these words were to be interpreted and what they really meant. Immediate access to the computer site was the major demand of the United States Once this was achieved in 1975, however, the United States threw a new ball into the game by suggesting that the Soviets would not live up to all the agreements, and therefore the United States wanted on-site monitoring by Americans.

In Moscow and in Dubna this new demand was not taken kindly, or lightly. There were angry words, especially at the scientific institute, suggesting that the United States had called

---

[2]This simply meant adding a second computing head onto the same memory bank and logic. There were protracted negotiations with the Soviets over the specifications and architecture of this computer—a normal practice in the United States, but one which had not occurred in the earlier negotiations. My analysis is that the Soviets, having acquired the previous two machines and having used them for several years, became rather sophisticated computer users in a reasonably short time and were thus able to enter into complex negotiations about the specifications and architecture of the newer model.

them liars even before they had an opportunity to demonstrate their trustworthiness. They were particularly incensed because they had completely abided by all of the agreements on the CDC 1604A's and 3600. In the United States, it was presumed that a more powerful computer exposed the Soviets to greater temptations to cheat on the agreement. A number of meetings were necessary to handle this new element that had been injected into the sale. A final resolution was reached when the Soviets agreed to pay for quarters, a living allowance, and the salary of an on-site American who would monitor the day-to-day activity at the computer site. After a significant period of silence following the last meeting when the details were worked out regarding the resident monitor, we received final approval from the Soviet side and then the U.S. side. One of the Soviet scientists told me later that the decision to allow an on-site monitor to be housed in Dubna on a permanent basis went to very high levels in the Soviet government. He did not elaborate on what "very high levels" meant.

*   *   *   *

After the order for that first CDC 1604A, discussions with GKNT (the State Committee of Science and Technology) produced an invitation from the Soviets for Control Data Corporation to participate in a computer exhibit in Moscow in May 1972. At that time we exhibited a CDC 3300 computer, as before with the official encouragement of the U.S. government, with then Secretary of State William Rogers participating in meetings with Soviet leaders to push for expanded trade. That was the beginning of a serious effort on the part of Control Data to obtain Soviet orders.

Among the new orders obtained was one from the Ministry of Geology for a CDC 3300, which, over a short time, underwent a series of upgrades.[3] One reason for these upgrades was that the rapidly advancing technology outstripped the licensing procedure. By the time we received a first license, the

---

[3]The 3300 was replaced with a 3600 and then a 6500 and finally upgraded to a Cyber 72 before the order was completely approved.

equipment had been superseded by the new technology and it was necessary to go back and renegotiate the contract with the Soviet Union. They were always concerned after the first purchase of the used CDC 1604A that they buy the latest technology and that the equipment be new.

Further discussions with GKNT, at the computer exhibition, caused CDC to issue an invitation to the Soviets to visit the United States for discussions of a comprehensive cooperation agreement. Under the terms of the agreement reached in 1973, Control Data and Soviet personnel agreed to work side by side on a number of projects. These included jointly developing a recursive computer that would be able to process blocks of data in any order (a new architectural concept); designing computer memories; developing and producing computer peripherals; researching and improving software; training computer specialists; finding new ways to apply computer technology to problems in medicine, education, meteorology, and physics, and solving production problems in manufacturing computer components. Control Data was to contribute much, but not all, of the technology; in these joint projects we intended to purchase some Soviet products and to participate in Soviet natural resource development. The Soviets, for their part, agreed to purchase a large number of Control Data peripheral products and computers.

Much care was taken to align this cooperative agreement with the long-term cooperation agreement signed between the two governments. Despite this alignment, some aspects of the agreement met with official roadblocks. The U.S. government would not agree to let Control Data participate in discussions necessary to start such projects as the joint development of computers or the designing of computer memories. We believed at Control Data that there was much new information obtainable in the architecture of both the memories and the computers; and while it is true we would have been providing them with technology that apparently was not readily available to them, we felt very strongly that we would be gaining access to technology in the architectures that we had not had an opportunity to develop. It had been Control Data's experience that we received as much benefit as we gave in these cooperative projects, and many times got *more* than we had given.

*   *   *   *

During the discussion of the cooperative agreement, Soviet representatives visited the United States. The delegation had included a first deputy vice-chairman of GKNT, a vice-minister from the Radio Ministry, a senior member of the State Planning Committee (GOSPLAN) at the vice-chairman level, and a number of very senior technical people from several of their more important institutes involved in computer research and development. The Soviets' visit to our company headquarters in the United States afforded us extensive opportunities to meet with these people in a focused, concentrated way over about a ten-day period, since they were in our charge the entire time they were here.

We talked about some joint ventures, but since they had no way of dealing with joint ventures, the idea was dropped. We spoke about transferring technology: building a factory and then sending some Control Data personnel to work in the factory for one to two years to insure that the techniques used in producing the computer equipment were properly assimilated into the environment in the Soviet Union. These discussions went well. It seemed as though our plan met with their approval.

It was not until some time later, after the agreement had been signed, when we were discussing a particular product for which an export license was required, that we discovered that our views were 180 degrees apart—their understanding of including outside professionals from the United States in the management, and our understanding of what those people would do in the management, were completely different. At one time, a very senior person from GKNT who had been involved in the discussions here in the United States told me bluntly, while we were *in his office* in the Soviet Union, that the Soviets would never agree to having any management personnel from the United States involved in the *management* of their factory in the Soviet Union. This was a big surprise to me in view of our past discussions. In thinking about that situation retrospectively, I realized that the first discussion in which we seemed to be in agreement took place in a *neutral* environment as far as the Soviets were concerned, with nobody accountable for, and no surveillance of, that discussion. But when the discussion took place in his office in the Soviet Union, it was likely that the conversation was recorded.

Further discussions on that particular subject caused me to believe that it is permissible to use certain words or develop certain ideas, or even to implement ideas to which they had objected, provided you couch the words or deeds in appropriate language. For instance, in some discussions relative to the educational components of our agreement, I suggested to one of the more senior members of GKNT that we would be pleased to work with them in solving their *problems* in education. My remark elicited a very strong response from him— for the next thirty minutes I got a lecture informing me that they didn't *have* any problems in their educational system. A very short time later, over a luncheon table in a restaurant, we got back on the same subject and the same gentleman suggested that he would be pleased to work with us in a cooperative way in the field of education. He was particularly interested in the uses of computers in education.

At that point, I realized the error of my ways. I had talked about "problems" in their educational system. There is a big difference between the word "problem" and the word "cooperation" in their perception of themselves. One can observe from this kind of interchange that the Soviets are very proud, and very sensitive about what they have accomplished in their system. Understandably, they do not like any criticism of the things they consider to be very significant accomplishments. They have developed a literate society from a relatively uneducated peasant population.

In certain areas and with certain people, one can be quite candid. I was driving my car with a member of the Council of Ministers here on a U.S. visit. There had been a newspaper report several days prior about the FBI apprehending and deporting a Russian visitor for spying, and it was reported by the newspaper that this deported individual belonged to the institute of which the person accompanying me was the director. I asked him in the car if this individual worked for him in his institute, and he said, "Certainly not. In spite of what you might read in the papers, I don't have those kinds of people in my employ." He said, "You know, in general, I feel that we get so little out of that kind of activity and it's such an embarrassment from time to time, that we ought to stop it altogether." And he added, "It might be useful if it could be stopped on both sides."

*   *   *   *

We concluded the fundamentals of the cooperative agreement after this visit to the United States and, after several more meetings, the final agreement was signed in late summer of 1973. When the cooperative agreement was concluded, all the documents that made up the agreement were turned over to the U.S. Department of Commerce for informational purposes, since there was no requirement at that time to file an export license application. We thought that since there was a long-term cooperative agreement between the U.S. and Soviet governments, our government would be very pleased to see such a cooperation agreement. Since the initial contacts had been made in 1972, it was my judgment at the time that this negotiation moved very rapidly and was signed in almost record time.

We set up a coordinating committee to administer the cooperation agreement between GKNT and Control Data. We started by having two meetings a year; one in Moscow and one in the United States. After five years, we cut it back to one meeting a year in alternating countries. Both parties were responsible for their own travel expenses to and from the country involved, but once they arrived in the meeting country the host paid for the travel and living expenses of the visiting party. We received the utmost courtesy during our visits to the Soviet Union.

One of the negotiations that was carried on between Control Data and the Ministry of Foreign Trade and GKNT involved work on the large-scale computer for the world meteorological project, to be used by the Hydrometeorological Center (Hydromet) in Moscow. Let me give you some short background on this particular negotiation. The World Meteorological Organization (WMO), a specialized agency of the United Nations based in Geneva, arranges exchanges of computer-processed observations of the weather and the ocean. It collects and transmits millions of bits of weather information every day from hundreds of observers around the world in an international code that is understood throughout the weather community. Three main centers exist—one in Melbourne, one in Washington, D.C., and one in Moscow. Of the three major centers, Hydromet in Moscow is the weakest link in the network because of its outmoded computing equipment. At the urging of the world weather community, and with the approval of the National Oceanographic and Atmospheric Administration (NOAA) in the United States, Control Data entered into an agreement in April 1975 to supply computer equipment and services to the Soviet Foreign Trade Office (Electronorgtechnica) for installation at the Hydromet offices in Moscow.

To meet the data processing demands of the center, a large computer was needed—a larger one than any we had shipped to the Soviets under previous contracts and one that considerably exceeded the guidelines of the NATO Coordinating Committee (COCOM) for export. Of the computers that we had previously shipped to the Ministry of Geology and the Ministry of Oil, the Cyber 172 came within COCOM guidelines and the Cyber 17 fell far below the cutoff. The machine chosen for Hydromet was the Cyber 76 with two satellite Cyber 17s. That machine, at that time, embodied ten-year-old technology, and some forty-five of the Cyber 76s had been sold worldwide. It was also used in cryptographic work by the U.S. National Security Agency.

We proceeded to complete the negotiation of the contract and to apply for the export license. We anticipated export license requirements for on-site monitoring for this large system. The Soviets agreed to all of this, including free access to the Hydromet Computer Center in Moscow. So the negotiations seemed to go rather well. Before the export license could be granted, however, some adverse publicity began building up because of leaks inside the U.S. government.

These leaks triggered a highly misleading column by Jack Anderson in the *Washington Post,* which pictured this $13 million electronic brain turning against the United States, tracking our own missiles, planes, and submarines, and decoding sensitive U.S. intelligence transmissions for the Soviets. Although Anderson was provided factual information about the computer, both before and after the article appeared, it did not prevent him from making a grossly biased presentation. His article, as one might guess, triggered negative speeches in Congress, which were printed in the Congressional Record; and Congress recommended that the export license not be granted. The license was then disallowed and Control Data suffered resulting financial losses.

Throughout this series of events, the Soviets remained quiet and reserved, but they kept pointing out that the computer was to be used not only for their own weather mapmaking and forecasting, but also for the Global Atmospheric Research Project (GARP). The project was to be completed that year, and the Soviets were planning to provide forty-five ships and a satellite to be put on various stations around the world to gather much of the project's data. They were very proud of their past participation in GARP efforts. Many times they had told me about some of the unusual places their ships had gone to gather data in preparation for the final year for the project. They were extremely disappointed, to say the least, when the export license was turned down.

To salvage something of the contract, we worked out an agreement to provide them a new system of much lesser capabilities, using four smaller computers of the size that we had previously shipped to the Soviet Union. The total cost of the revised project turned out to be about the same as the cost for the original project, although the revised equipment was much less capable. The new contracts were worked out rapidly, and we applied for an export license for the first of the series of four computers that were to take the place of the Cyber 76. We received rapid approval from the Department of Commerce. We shipped the first computer and got it installed and operational. The second computer, its export license approved, was in the air freight terminal in Frankfurt, West

Germany, en route to the Soviet Union when President Carter declared the embargo against the Soviet Union for their actions in Afghanistan. We tried for several months to get that computer released and on its way to the Soviet Union to fulfill the contract, but we were not successful.

It is worth noting the rather unusual situation relative to the payment for the computer. The Soviets had made a major down payment on all four of the computer systems in advance of the shipment. Of course they paid in full for the one that was installed in Moscow and would have paid in full for the second computer had it not been stopped at the Frankfurt airport. I tried a number of times to get them to cancel the orders, since we held their money in escrow but, for reasons that I have yet to understand, they refused to cancel these orders. Some years later they decided that they should collect some interest on that money and applied to Control Data to either send the money back or pay interest on it. Control Data, at that point, agreed that they would send the money back. The order has still not been cancelled.

After the Cyber 76 order was turned down, the negotiations on GARP[4] began to go badly. The Soviets withdrew their offer of forty-five ships for the project. I believe some time later they did put some ships into the project, but it was a very limited number compared to the original forty-five. The Soviet response to these actions on the part of the United States government was to withdraw from many other aspects of GARP, which had a desultory effect on the entire project when it was finished.

*   *   *   *

Concurrently with Control Data's work on the developmental projects and the sale of computing equipment to the Soviet Union, under other terms of our cooperation agreement we were to consider what could be purchased from the Soviet Union. One such item was greeting cards to be produced by

---

[4]The World Meteorological Organization, the United States and the Soviet Union, plus numerous other countries, held negotiations and discussions relative to what was to be accomplished in the final year (1979) of the Global Atmospheric Research Project.

Soviet presses and labor, with paper supplied by Finland, and then sold in Germany and the United Kingdom. One difficulty was that the Soviets always wanted a price that was the same as the world market price. This brought on long, involved discussions in which I had to say, "No, that's the price you see in the gift card shop and not the price that we are going to pay you. Somebody has to pay for the transportation, the warehousing, and the selling of these greeting cards to the various dealers, and each party in the chain will take its own expenses as the cards make their way into the Western market. But you must produce them for a price that is about 50 percent less than the price you would see in the gift shop and, in many cases, even less than that."

We arranged an agreement with the Soviets to buy shotguns and sell them through dealers in the United States. This worked out reasonably well, except that they never could understand that guns are a seasonable item and that when they agree to a shipment date they have to deliver on that date or the guns wind up in an inventory for the following year. We eventually had to terminate that agreement because they never made on-time deliveries, although the quality was always excellent. We also bought books—art books mostly—to be sold in the United States.

In the course of these discussions to buy Soviet products, the question was never resolved as to whether the products would be countertrade credits for other things that Control Data sold to the Soviet Union.[5] As it turned out, countertrade was something the Soviets could not handle internally. The Ministry of Foreign Trade had a small section at one time devoted to countertrade projects, but it was extremely ineffective. Moreover, one ministry would not agree with another ministry that foreign trade credits should be given. Many of the ministries were not even concerned about countertrade credits, even though countertrade was in their area of responsi-

---

[5]Countertrade credits are simply a way to balance the trade between two business entities or between two countries. It is common practice for one country, especially in East Europe, to buy something from the United States if the United States will buy from them an equivalent amount, or some percentage of what they are buying from the United States.

bility. Once they were given the budget in hard currency to buy the products they wanted, they ignored whether or not any countertrade was ever brought to bear on the product acquisition. Likewise, the Soviet foreign trade export organization concerned did not have any real interest in making the countertrade agreement work. They were simply selling things that they wanted to sell anyway. It never occurred to them that the sale of those items would be useful in increasing the amount of hard currency available for buying needed items outside of the country.

There was one major countertrade project that would surely have been successful had it not been for the intrusion of extraneous events, and which further illustrates practical human relations considerations important to effective interchange with the Soviets. The Hermitage Museum in Leningrad had access to a multiple user computer system that Control Data had sold to the Academy of Sciences. The Hermitage wanted to use a computer system to catalogue some 3½ million items in their warehouses. These artifacts and artworks had never been on display in the museum. The Soviets planned to design a cataloging system that could be used in cooperation with other museums in Europe. The heart of the project was to be a catalogue language, for use in the computer systems, that could describe items to others. So the Hermitage management asked Control Data to think of ways in which the museum could earn some hard currency to buy its own computer system.

After preliminary discussions, Control Data proposed that the Hermitage put together an exhibition of Hermitage artifacts and artworks to send to the United States and be placed on exhibit in six major U.S. museums. Various books, models, miniatures, and reproductions of paintings would be produced by the USSR and sold through the museum bookstores and through some mail-order channels to earn the hard currency for their computer purchase. The admission fees charged by the museums for viewing the exhibition were to cover the cost of displaying the exhibition. These revenues were to be kept for the museums' own accounts, with none going to the Soviets. The Ministry of Culture had the final approval on all of the arrangements for this very large exhibition—estimated value $115 million. Some of the artifacts, such as the Scythian Gold, were said to be priceless.

It is important in dealing with the Soviets to be conscious of their sensitivity to the symmetry of positions. Several times I requested meetings for my staff with various individuals in the Ministry of Culture. In a number of cases the individual we wished to call on refused to meet with the staff member I had designated because he believed his position in the Soviet hierarchy was somewhat above that of the Control Data staff member. When I personally asked for meetings, I had no trouble meeting with the first deputy minister of culture, but I was never successful in meeting with the minister of culture. When meetings were required between the museum staff of the Hermitage and museum staff members in the United States, it had to be director of one museum to director of the other museum—and so on down the line. This was true in many of the other dealings and negotiations we had with the Soviets, but more so at the Ministry of Culture than at any other organization that I have dealt with in the Soviet Union.

The negotiations at the Ministry of Culture finally culminated in an agreement in which the exhibition was to begin in May 1980 at the National Gallery of Art in Washington, D.C. The Soviets were extremely pleased by this opportunity and very proud of having that large exhibition opening in Washington.

We had applied to have the exhibit granted "freedom from legal seizure" through the United States Information Agency (USIA) and were awaiting the approval of that application when the Soviet troops moved into Afghanistan in December 1979. In January 1980 the State Department refused to grant the freedom from legal seizure. At that point the entire project had to be cancelled because the Soviets refused to ship their treasures into the United States without the guarantee. Control Data had to undo many things that it had started, such as the printing of catalogues and the making of art reproductions and replicas of the Scythian Gold and other valuables.

The Ministry of Culture was so intrigued by this method of art exchange that the first deputy minister of culture at one time told me that they intended to do all of their art exchanges in that fashion in the future. I do not believe that has actually occurred, but they did feel that it was an acceptable way to proceed with art exchanges. They held open the possibility of doing the Hermitage exhibition in the United States for two years after the original application for relief from legal seizure was denied. Since it was never possible to get the new administration to agree that we should have a Hermitage exhibition, the entire project was finally cancelled, much to their disappointment. Because the Soviets are a very proud people and feel that they have some wonderful art galleries in the Soviet Union, they would naturally like very much to share them with the world.

*   *   *   *

In 1975 I became associated with the American Committee on East-West Accord. This is a distinguished group of Americans headed by John Kenneth Galbraith, George Kennan and Donald Kendall. As a member of this committee, I was invited with four others from the committee to visit the Soviet Union. During that visit I had the opportunity to meet many people outside the business sphere of influence. The American Committee is interested in better relations between the United States and the Soviet Union and has always supported détente, arms control, and trade. Many of the people that I met through the American Committee were instrumental in arranging meetings for me with many of the ministries with which I wanted to do business. Because of the aims of the American Committee and the discussions that were carried on with these people outside of the business sphere, I believe that the Soviets came to feel that I could be trusted.

These early contacts through the association with the American Committee led to other meetings, such as "Vienna I" in November 1974, which was chaired by George Ball in an attempt to get a better relationship between the two countries established. There were many European countries represented at Vienna I and these discussions were continued with "Vienna II" in March 1979. Eventually they turned into a new committee, New Initiatives for East-West Relations. There were many new acquaintances and contacts with Soviets that were a result of these meetings. These new people afforded other opportunities for further discussions with new ministries interested in trade.

Through my work with GKNT, I also became involved with the International Institute of Applied Systems Analysis (IIASA) in Laxenburg, Austria, a high-level research-oriented group with members from the United States, the Soviet Union, Western and Eastern Europe. The association and interchange with the Soviet scientists who were resident at IIASA was helpful and useful in arranging meetings with various institutes and scientists in the Soviet Union. I find the work conducted at Laxenburg particularly interesting because one can observe the scientists from the United States, the Soviet Union, and Europe working together in a mixed environment. I do not know of any other institution like IIASA anywhere else in the world.

*   *   *   *

The last point that I would like to discuss has to do with what is sometimes called back-channel negotiations. A number of times I was told by some persons in the Soviet Union that they thought it might be important for me to carry back certain ideas, primarily on trade issues such as the grain embargo and the building of electronic factories. Sometimes I was asked to take back to the United States certain suggestions that they thought should be passed on to official channels. In the early seventies I had people say to me, "Well, I don't know why you business people don't tell your government what you would really like regarding this or that situation." The Soviets seemed to believe that the United States and the Soviet Union must be organized along the same lines; they did not quite understand why our enterprises do not function exactly like their enterprises.

It is hard to describe to them the differences as we see them between two societies—the structures that flow from democracy and capitalism and those that flow from communism. I have always told them that I do *not* represent the U.S. government—that anything that I might bring back at their request or any request that I might make of them would have nothing to do with the position of the U.S. government. And, in fact, sometimes my views might be contrary to the U.S. government's position.

However, despite my protestations, they do seem to view this back-channel information as important. Many times it can influence how they look at a particular idea or project. For instance, I was allowed to look at many of their computer factories and many of their component factories, and to visit a great many of their institutes. At one point the minister of electronics told me that he hoped all these visits would help to establish in the minds of the U.S. government that the Soviet Union is not a backward country, but had the capability of doing many of its own scientific investigations and taking care of many of its own manufacturing requirements. Nevertheless, he went on to inform me, the Soviet Union was such a vast country and so spread out that they have difficulty in manufacturing enough of anything to meet their requirements. This, of course, was expected to be passed on to appropriate people in the U.S. government, which I subsequently did.

For all its warts and calluses, trade with the Soviet Union can be and is exciting and rewarding. The business negotiations that go with trade can severely test your business skills, as well as your creativity and imagination. My dealings with the Soviets as people have always reinforced my thinking that people are people almost wherever you go. My dealings with the Soviets as a society taught me to look at many things in different ways. Nevertheless it is my conclusion that, while they are proud, hard bargainers, it is possible to do business with them, to sign binding agreements that are mutually beneficial and, withal, to make a profit.

Appendix: Data on Equipment

MODEL	INTRODUCED	MEMORY CAPACITY	SPEED
CDC 1604A	April 1958	160K bytes	0.12 MIPS
CDC 3300	November 1965	262K bytes	0.17 MIPS
CDC 3600	January 1964	192K bytes	0.45 MIPS
CDC 6400	December 1964	1 megabyte	1.20 MIPS
CDC 6500	March 1967	1 megabyte	2.00 MIPS
CDC 660	July 1962	1 megabyte	3.00 MIPS
CYBER 17	October 1965	96K bytes	.10 MIPS
CYBER 76	March 1971	.5 megabyte	15.00 MIPS
CYBER 172	April 1974	2 megabytes	0.80 MIPS

Units used:

MIPS = millions of instructions per second
1 megabyte = 1,000K bytes

7

Discussing Nuclear Issues and Trade Relations

Jeanne Vaughn Mattison

T
HE SKEPTICISM of friends and colleagues was understandable. After all, you don't just have a brief conversation with the Soviet ambassador at the Soviet
embassy about a proposed trip to Moscow to discuss the
reduction of nuclear weapons and the advancement of East-
West trade and then start packing.

Add to the equation a request to see high-level officials at a
policymaking level, a preferred time schedule, with a yet-to-be
determined composition of the American delegation, and you
have an unlikely prescription for a successful outcome.

Yet the need was urgent. This was November 1983. With
American-Soviet relations seemingly frozen, it was an appropriate time for the Washington-based American Committee
on East-West Accord to weigh in with a senior delegation to
engage in candid discussions—discussions wherein both parties might receive, sound out, and explore productive and
practical measures of a problem-solving nature to enhance
East-West trade and to reduce political tensions and lessen the
possibility of nuclear confrontation.

The program described in this essay was assisted by the Ploughshares Fund of San
Francisco. In May 1986, subsequent to the events recounted in this chapter, the
American Committee on East-West Accord changed its name to the American
Committee on U.S.-Soviet Relations.

We did not wish to impinge on traditional diplomatic discourse nor try to make policy. To avoid this, we maintained close contact with the State Department and, as we progressed, with the National Security Council. We thought we could be useful. We were unofficial and therefore free of institutional positions, attitudes, and expectations, and certain observances of protocol. We had in hand a well-developed set of comprehensive proposals that were balanced, sensible, verifiable, and in the interest of both countries. The proposals were politically viable, the timing propitious, and the opportunities at hand.

Ambassador Anatoliy Dobrynin evidently came to a similar determination. A long discussion on the substance of the proposed talks concluded with a suggestion to begin consultations with his staff, working out guidelines and details.

Notwithstanding the validity of our agenda, the credentials and credibility of the American Committee itself, and the seriousness of our purpose, the intangible but discernible element all along was reason. Given the U.S.-Soviet stalemate, and the prospect of worsening relations, some minimum form of communication was needed—some open line that was alive and functioning, some conduit pending a more hopeful day.

Careful Preparations Are Essential

From the beginning, we sought to avoid duplicating the efforts of other exchange programs and said so directly. If another, established exchange was considered to be an equally appropriate forum, then why institute a new and untried exchange? As it was, we held course and continued to map out arrangements for a joint exchange between the USSR Academy of Sciences and the American Committee on East-West Accord, with agreement on a reciprocal visit.

Another concern was to avoid the debilitating rhetoric that characterizes so many exchanges. We made this point with the Soviets, and it was remembered during our actual exchanges in Moscow. Time and opportunity were put to good use.

Final preparations mostly concerned the time-consuming coordination of schedules and availability of participants (with their delegation, as well as ours), discussion on reciprocation, duration of visit, official and institutional host, financial arrangements, flight schedules, interpreters, and, always, the shifting political winds.

Though each of these areas required good will, patience, and cooperation on both sides, the more subtle issues were the more interesting and challenging.

How best to deal with the asymmetrical aspects of the delegations? We were private citizens; the Soviets, officials. Had we not expressed many times over our desire to see senior officials from the Politburo, Central Committee and scientific institutes, the problem of asymmetry would not have been so severe. A solution was worked out—that we meet in Moscow and not elsewhere, and that the American delegation be as senior as possible. Yet no matter how prestigious or how influential the composition of the American delegation, we were still private citizens representing individual views—some coinciding with official U.S. policy, some not.

How best to protect against the vulnerability of that very luxury of expression and freedom? Here surely was a classic example of the dichotomy of the systems and the complexities therein. This, too, was discussed openly and frankly both with Soviet officials from the embassy and with senior officials from Moscow who sought consultations with committee officials here in Washington. We came to a clear and specific understanding: that beyond informing our respective governments, substantive discussions would not be made public. We declared that in no way should our delegation be viewed as necessarily representative of the views of our government. By thus clarifying the frame of reference, by attempting to anticipate as much as possible any potential for embarrassment to individuals, to the delegation as a whole, or to either government, we created a healthy environment for candid discourse based on mutuality of purpose.

In our preparations, we articulated minimum but important ground rules, which were honored. But even more important, something else was at work here. We were working the problem, not each other; looking for answers, not adversaries; dealing with reality, not mind-set.

Our attention was focused on nuclear weapons, security, and economics, particularly East-West trade. We had a team who knew about such things: Robert McNamara, former secretary of defense; U.S.-Soviet specialist Professor Seweryn Bialer of Columbia University; Dr. Carson Mark, former director of the Theoretical Division of Los Alamos Scientific Laboratory; Admiral Noel Gayler, former commander-in-chief of all Pacific forces and former director of the National Security Agency; Robert Schmidt, chairman of Earth Energy Systems and president of the American Committee on East-West Accord; and myself, director of the committee.

We had arranged in addition for a key Republican and a key Democratic senator to join us, but a last-minute budget vote kept them in Washington.

Our host for the discussions and leader of the Soviet delegation was Academician Yevgeniy P. Velikhov, vice president of the USSR Academy of Sciences. Three other bearers of the academician designation also received the American Committee delegation: Roald Sagdeyev, director of the Space Research Institute; Georgiy Arbatov, director of the USA-Canada Institute; and President of the Academy of Sciences Anatoliy Aleksandrov.

The invitation from Velikhov was hard fought and hard won. From the very beginning of my discussions with Soviet embassy officials, it was my task diplomatically to "suggest" a preference of institutional and individual host. Not surprisingly, I received diplomatic "suggestions" in return—all at lower levels of officialdom. My best counter was truth and the reality of the situation: I explained, as they knew, that I could not possibly put together a very high-level and influential delegation unless the invitation from Moscow was equivalent.

I had met Velikhov before in the States, knew that he was one of the Soviet Union's top physicists, if not *the* top physicist, and noted his close association with the most senior Soviet officials. (A short time before we left for Moscow, in fact, Velikhov accompanied Gorbachev to London just before Gorbachev's ascension to power.) Additionally, within the prestigious USSR Academy of Sciences, Velikhov headed up a little known but very important subcommittee of scientists whose purpose was to consider how to avert nuclear war.

Here, then, was a handle on the aforementioned problem of asymmetry. A key factor in the preliminary discussions concerning our institutional host was knowing from the start what we needed and wanted, and convincing them that we were serious people, with serious proposals, wanting serious discussions. I myself felt judged on this from the very inception of the request to the day of departure. I am grateful for the opportunities and cooperation accorded the delegation both from our own government and from the Soviet Union.

In essence, we were in an enviable position. We were not participating in official negotiations, so there were no preconditions or positions, no mind-set, no procedural framework, no constraints, no points to win, no bargaining chips to trade, no face to save. Our only aim was to examine options and to move towards resolutions.

Outline of a Productive Visit

In February 1985, our delegation was received in Moscow with every courtesy consistent with our unofficial status—one could even say, royally. We arrived on a Saturday and had set aside Sunday for rest and orientation. To our surprise, and subsequent delight, we were invited to Zagorsk, about an hour from Moscow, to visit with the Patriarch and Bishop of the historic monastery of the Russian Orthodox Church. The visit was memorable and especially useful politically in that the car trip itself provided an interesting opportunity to meet informally and to exchange views and ideas with Soviet scientists who accompanied us. Immediately, relationships were personalized and topics aired for priority—a prologue.

Throughout our stay, the American Committee delegation held meetings, both formal and informal, with senior Soviet scientists and nuclear arms–control authorities. While retaining the confidentiality of the outcome of the discussions, it may be helpful to outline our stated objectives and agenda for the purpose of sharing material and processes for possible use by others involved in such exchanges.

To anyone familiar with U.S.-Soviet discussions, the one thing Soviets appreciate is specificity. This I learned from Ambassador W. Averell Harriman when he helped organize the American Committee on East-West Accord in 1977. Another extremely important experience passed on to me by American experts on the Soviet Union is that informal coffee breaks, toasts, or personal asides can be as informative as the actual on-the-record deliberations.

Here then is the gist of our agenda, reiterated many times in person during our preparatory meetings to a large number of Soviet officials in the Soviet embassy in Washington and to representatives from Moscow:

Objectives

The primary objective of the talks is to explore with competent and influential Soviets the ways in which the probability of nuclear war can be reduced by the coordinate actions of the U.S. and the USSR.

We expect discussions to be free of polemics and devoted to examination, in an impartial way, of the potential of the various options towards this end. We expect both to talk and to listen.

We wish to discuss comprehensively with the Soviets certain promising proposals already submitted to the United States government for consideration. At the same time, we wish to give opportunity to the Soviets to unveil ideas of their own towards our common objective.

We wish further to explore the Soviet reaction to comprehensive and synergistic actions, as opposed to meager and uncoordinated steps in the nuclear weapons area.

Agenda

For our part, we wish to discuss five questions that we believe should inform our nuclear relationship:

    a. Do nuclear weapons have sensible military use?

b. Can security against nuclear attack be gained by unilateral action?
c. Does either the USA or the USSR possess or appear to
   be moving toward a first strike capability?
d. Given political will on both sides, are there substantive
   political or security obstacles to a general settlement of
   nuclear issues?
e. Should nuclear agreements be linked to other issues
   between us, or may they be resolved on their own
   merits?

We wish to discuss eight proposals which, in our view have
the potential to reduce to negligible proportions the potential of
nuclear war between us:

1. Abandon, on both sides, hostile rhetoric and the im-
   plicit assumption that war is inevitable.
2. Formally abandon nuclear war–fighting doctrines on
   both sides.
3. Broaden communication and exchanges of every kind,
   including economic policies which promote nonstra-
   tegic U.S. and Soviet trade.
4. Establish as the objective of nuclear arms negotiations
   increasing the stability of deterrence at minimum force
   levels. Would a mutual, renewable moratorium on the
   development, testing or deployment of new weapons
   systems contribute to this?
5. Ban "dedicated" anti-satellite weapons and all other
   space-based weapons—adhere to all provisions of the
   ABM Treaty.
6. Evaluate processes for deep and continuing cuts in
   nuclear warheads and nuclear weapons–grade
   material.
7. Establish verifiable nuclear weapons–free zones in
   areas of potential conflict, while at the same time
   redeploying potentially threatening conventional
   forces.
8. Develop broad and effective measures for the cooperation of the superpowers and the other nuclear weapons states to inhibit the spread of nuclear weapons
   worldwide.

Our visit was capped by a meeting with Foreign Minister
Andrei Gromyko—who extended an hour's appointment into
a two hour and forty minute conversation.

Our delegation both briefed and was debriefed by U.S. officials in the Department of State, the National Security Council, and the American embassy, before and after the meetings. We were of course scrupulous—as were Soviet counterparts—not to get into the specifics of any upcoming intergovernmental negotiations.

Our deliberations concluded not only with an agreement to hold a reciprocal meeting in Washington as planned, but additionally both sides agreed in principle to conduct joint studies on specific issues of mutual interest—ground-breaking studies as yet not undertaken by either government or institute. The American Committee undertook to nominate potential topics for this purpose and is currently developing outlines of the collaborative studies.

The Soviets reciprocated with serious discussion of real issues, remarkably free of polemics. No official assurances were given or sought, but an attitude of reason and openness prevailed.

If ideas lead to action, and we hold that they do, this initiative of the American Committee on East-West Accord will surely contribute toward a more pragmatic relationship with the Soviet Union. Our prescription for the future: more of the same, tailored in reason and animated by conviction.

8

Negotiating on the Academic Front

Valentina G. Brougher

I N THE FALL of 1979, I traveled to the Soviet Union with an executive administrator from the Council on International Educational Exchange (CIEE) for two weeks of negotiations with Leningrad State University and with Central Sputnik, the state agency in Moscow that handles all travel arrangements for foreign students. We were entrusted with the task of working out a new five-year agreement that would allow the Cooperative Russian Language Program at Leningrad State University (summer, semester, and academic year) to continue into its third decade.

Our goal was to work out the best possible arrangements both for the academic component of the program (daily classes, lectures, films) and the cultural component (local excursions and weekend trips, theater tickets, meetings with youth, special visits to factories and collective farms, and a field trip to several other Soviet republics). We would meet with university officials to discuss housing and academic arrangements, then fly to Moscow to review the cultural part of the program and discuss travel dates and arrangements with Central Sputnik. A protocol of agreement would ultimately be signed both by Leningrad University administrators and Central Sputnik directors in Moscow.

The CIEE Russian program in 1979 was already part of an

established tradition, both for the Soviet side and for the American colleges and universities comprising the Russian Consortium within CIEE. Nevertheless, we headed for the USSR with the usual basic concerns: the availability and location of dormitories, the number and quality of excursions, the supply of printed teaching materials, and the like. A number of summers before this negotiating trip, I had served as the American faculty member, or group leader, in charge of thirty or so students—one-fifth of the total group studying in the summer at Leningrad. I thus could speak from personal observations about the program's strengths and weaknesses. And as fate would have it, four years later, in 1983, I was to serve as resident director of the whole summer program and to refer a number of times to our agreement, when the Soviet side was "not sure" what we were entitled to.

Sitting around a large table in one of the university's large meeting rooms, facing the university vice-president, a number of deans and assistant deans, and the obligatory representative from the university's Foreign Department (Inotdel), I wondered which of these men (there were no women on the Soviet side) had dealt with the program before, which would be most supportive of the program, and which would be least likely to be influenced by the post-détente tensions between our countries. It was also apparent that they were wondering what to expect from us.

My colleague from CIEE had come for such negotiations many times over the years and had earned the reputation of being a talented negotiator. Since he usually came accompanied by an established male professor from one of the consortium universities, my presence, to some extent, must have surprised them. One may hear a lot of rhetoric about the equality of women in the Soviet Union, but it is a fact of Soviet life that almost all positions of power and trust are still assigned to men. To have a relatively young woman speaking for a large consortium visibly puzzled but also intrigued them.

After a few mornings and afternoons of discussions, reviewing our concerns and voicing suggestions for the future, a number of observations about the whole process—and the factors that come into play at such nonofficial, nongovernmental discussions—began to take shape in my mind almost subconsciously.

Structural Differences

Although one expects government-level negotiations to involve strict adherence to established protocol, it was somewhat of a surprise to note that, even in a university setting, the form, progress, and atmosphere of our discussions had a very formal, "official" stamp to them. The hierarchy of power at the table was observed very strictly by the Soviet side. An associate dean did not allow himself to respond first to an issue, even if the issue at hand had direct bearing on his office and he was the most knowledgeable person on that issue. It was his superior, the dean, who set the tone and signaled the direction the Soviet response would take. Once the person in power had made his point, others simply remained silent or offered only supportive comments.

I noted only a few, isolated instances when we had any inkling of a difference of opinion among the Soviet representatives. At one point, an assistant dean offered a brief history of the program's existence and success at the university as an indirect way of supporting the program's continuation in Leningrad. The suggestion had been made by one of the more powerful deans that perhaps we "would be happier in Moscow." In an American university setting, not only would such restraint and indirectness be unusual, but a consistently united front would not be maintained for long. Put a few American deans together, and no matter how much they might try to reflect their university's policy and attitudes, differences of opinion, of approach, would surface quite quickly.

When a Soviet administrator was merely silent, did we take this to be an automatic indication that he was low on the rung of power at the table? Of course not. As has been pointed out many times by various people, the person who is silent at such private negotiations may wield great power within the party apparatus. He may in fact have been assigned the task of sitting in at the meetings and observing how carefully his colleagues are adhering to agreed-upon guidelines. That is part of the mystery and challenge of dealing with the Soviets.

A Soviet university, like all enterprises in the USSR, is state owned and thus answerable to the city and state governments, which means ultimately to Moscow. Whatever commitments university officials make must not in any way run counter to the policy line set by the Kremlin, the Ministry of Higher Education, and other such government institutions. In 1979, with détente relegated to the recent past, we sensed that any substantive changes we wanted in the way the program was divided between the university and Sputnik would probably meet with opposition; the gentlest of feelers about the university's resources indicated that this was not the time to try to change the basic structure.

Americans, moreover, were clearly in disfavor now. At times, cold but polite comments were punctuated with the refrain, "It's not a time of détente, you know," implying that if détente had continued, they would and could have made more of an effort to be flexible. "Other groups are in greater favor now," one official openly said to us in Moscow, as we argued for more guaranteed days in Moscow and more interesting field trips. In the same vein, a university official indicated that the development of new teaching aids could not move ahead quickly because the scholars involved were committed first of all to designing materials for the French and Italians, who were "in a stronger position now."

Like others from the private sector trying to do business in the USSR, we were constantly being reminded of the role the political climate plays in talks with Soviets. Even if some of the individuals we dealt with may have had a more flexible attitude privately, they were bound by "the spirit of the times." We understood that to act against this spirit, set by the party and the state, would have been a dangerous and foolhardy course for any of them to follow.

Another factor in the way our discussions progressed was the Soviet system of centralized planning. It was at least partly responsible for the rigidity and inflexibility university and Sputnik officials displayed on a number of issues. In America, even state universities, dependent as they are on the state for their financial resources, assume the major responsibility for their development. It was thus somewhat difficult to adjust to the idea that a university is not in charge of its life and resources, but is in fact bound up in the various five-year plans drawn up for the city, the republic (Russian Soviet Federated Socialist Republic, in the case of Leningrad), and the Soviet Union as a whole. In fact, a Soviet university not only functions on the basis of such plans but is at their mercy.

To give a concrete example, one of the questions to which we immediately addressed ourselves was the availability of dormitory (as opposed to hotel) space for our students. To our question about housing, the university vice-president, in a cold, official tone, announced that the dormitory our groups had stayed in before would soon be closing for "major repairs," and that we would be assigned a hotel. We stressed that it was very important to all universities concerned that the students be housed in a university dormitory for the total experience of studying and living in a Soviet university. As we exchanged comments, it became clear that the university would have an easier time housing us in a Sputnik hotel for a number of reasons. We were told that dorm allocations are entered into the various plans the university prepares, and consequently there was little flexibility. Some dorms, they added, were approved for use only by groups from socialist countries. Finally, because we kept pressing for dormitory space, they offered one or two dorms as "a possibility," but emphasized that they were located "too far from the university" and might not be "suitable" for our students. American students tended to be too critical and demanding, was their explanation. We pressed to be allowed to see these "possible" dormitories, although from the reluctant tone in which they had been offered, we suspected that in fact they would not do. (They did turn out to be in an undesirable location and inadequate to our needs).

We asked when our old favorite would have its repairs completed. Was it a matter of a year or two, or more? The explanation offered was vague, but ultimately honest. They pointed out that all they knew was that money had been set aside in the city budget for the repairs, which were scheduled to begin as soon as the students had finished the academic year in June. But, they added, it was difficult to guarantee that the work would proceed on schedule. It would depend on the availability of men and equipment, i.e., on the other projects in the city plan being completed by projected deadlines. And then, who could predict how long the necessary repairs would take? Perhaps the dormitory would require more work than visible to the eye, etc. The university officials were tacitly recognizing not only their powerlessness before city plans but also Soviet inefficiency in carrying out the plans' objectives.

To summarize, one normally expects a certain amount of vagueness in talking about the future. But in a Soviet setting such vagueness may or may not necessarily be due to a conscious desire to be noncommittal. At times, it may in fact reflect the true state of affairs when it is a question of state/city resources and planning.

As we continued our discussions into the second week—and even made a quick trip to Moscow to go over the outline of excursions and cities—it became clear that both rigidity and a kind of procrastination were also due to the role Soviet administrators play in private negotiations. My colleague and I had come to the table fully empowered to speak for the full membership of the Russian consortium. We had been entrusted by our colleagues to sign an agreement that would reflect the structure and standards worked out through many years, both at the biannual meetings of the full membership and on all negotiating trips. The Soviet side undoubtedly had internal meetings before coming to the table; they must have had their discussions about the program relative to the goals of Leningrad State University and the political realities of the time. But it was also clear that they had come to our discussions with a certain prepared position on the basic issues in question. Comparing their position on day one on the question of the structure of the year-long program or the number of students we could send on the semester program with that of a week later, nothing much seemed to have changed.

Their rigidity seemed to indicate a careful adherence to established guidelines. On a few issues, interestingly enough, such as increasing the size of the total group in the summer, we were told that they could not give us an immediate answer but would have "to think about it and discuss it again." We took this as a signal that they themselves might not have a problem with our request but could not act independently without checking with some authorities, like the Ministry of Education or Central Sputnik.

Perhaps because we Westerners tend to be relatively impatient or to prefer direct, clear signals, vagueness and noncommitment for longer periods than we would expect seemed particularly striking at our discussions. Nevertheless, it was transparent that, beyond the reasons suggested above, people with whom we dealt persisted in being vague also as a way of keeping us guessing and forcing us to return repeatedly to the same issues. This gave them a good opportunity to observe what was especially important to us, what we would strive to press, and what we might let slide.

Moreover, we sensed that the Soviet side consciously practiced vagueness and noncommitment as a way of driving home the message that it is the foreigner that finds himself in the position of the supplicant. "You will have to live up to our demands, not we to yours," seemed to be the nonverbalized message they liked to send out. We consciously tried to counter this by pointing out the mutual benefits of such a program as ours for both sides. The program meant a good amount of much-needed hard currency for the Soviet Union. Moreover, having American groups studying in Leningrad added a certain amount of prestige to Leningrad University (university rivalry is not limited to the West). Although we did not throw out these observations the minute the Soviet side played the tune "this program may be more trouble than it is worth to us," we did voice them in polite diplomatic language when we wanted them to know that we considered ourselves not supplicants but equal partners in a business arrangement.

After all, if the Soviet Union did not see great benefits from having our groups study in the country, the program would not be allowed to exist and we would not be sitting around a table discussing the business arrangements in a five-year protocol of agreement.

Cultural Factors

The factors discussed above, which have their roots in the nature of the Soviet political system and economy, were not the only ones at play in the dynamics of dealing with Soviets. There were other factors which could be labeled "cultural differences" or grouped under a heading, such as, "How Russians/Soviets differ from Americans."

The appearance of coffee, cognac, chocolates as early as 10:00 A.M. was the rule rather than the exception. Particularly on the first day, toasts from both sides were part of the required protocol. We drank to peace and friendship, to the city of Leningrad and the university, to the program and its future, to students and teachers, etc. Any American not used to making toasts, and even learning to be a bit flowery and longwinded, would find himself most uncomfortable. The Soviets have a lot of respect for anyone who has a way with words; it signals to them a worthy opponent.

Although it is a common human tendency to defend one's country the moment a foreigner/outsider attacks it, the Soviets are particularly sensitive about any remarks that they feel criticize their way of life. In discussing any shortcomings of the previous years, such as inadequate toilet facilities, old uncomfortable buses, and poor evening meals, we had to be extremely careful not to sound like critical Americans who were used to higher standards. As anyone who has spent any time in the USSR knows, the Soviets are quickly offended by any comments that they think are made to point out the shortcomings in their system. This is partly because the more worldly and traveled among them are themselves more than aware of the problems, partly because any foreigner's reminder, however unconscious or indirect, of their lagging behind the West in any way is immediately translated into a socio-political comparison and confrontation between the socialist and capitalist systems.

Thus, when we had to bring to their attention the unappetizing suppers provided our students, we first focused on the positive aspects of the cafeteria service, and then made suggestions. Breakfasts were good—there is nothing like cream of wheat, cooked in milk and sugar, with hot butter on top, we pointed out. But then, we added, understanding that it is difficult to feed such a large group of students, some of whom were rather finicky and difficult to please at that, couldn't something be done to make the suppers more interesting? How about more of those cheese fritters that the students liked, and less reheated rice? There certainly would have been no point in issuing such an ultimatum as: "We have a contract. We pay you good money. Now please provide." The Russians would not only be quick to cry *"Kak vy nas obizhaete!"* (How insulting!), but would stubbornly refuse to do anything to remedy the situation.

Americans as a people tend to smile more than Russians. It is part of our "social" face. Russians tend to smile only when something especially pleasant/happy or witty/humorous has occurred or been said. At other times they sit with what to an American seem like cold, indifferent faces, at times seemingly projecting anger and/or hostility. This was indeed the case at our meetings. We had to keep reminding ourselves that just because they were not smiling pleasantly at us most of the time did not mean that they were indifferent or angry or hostile. They were behaving perfectly naturally. On the other hand, when someone would begin to smile or laugh good-naturedly, we knew that our words were being well received. When our own smiles and humor produced no changes in somber Russian faces, we knew we had a long way to go.

There was yet another crucial difference in the behavior of our Soviet administrators and representatives. Americans who represent their universities or firms have trained themselves to pursue their objectives both firmly and politely. To lose one's temper at the negotiating table, to allow oneself a temper tantrum, no matter how provoked, is to be a poor, weak negotiator. From what could be observed at our meetings both in Leningrad and Moscow, that is not always the case with Soviets. There were times when a Soviet official would get angry and sarcastic, when he would lose his temper, raise his voice, shout. A Sputnik high official behaved precisely in this way when he accused some students of being interested "in things other than their studies." And a university dean lost his temper when asked about a mixup in travel dates the spring before.

It could be argued that the Soviet negotiator is consciously allowing himself to lose his temper as a way not only of demonstrating how strongly he feels about an issue but also, perhaps, of openly flaunting his power over the foreigner. Though that may be the case at times, the following might also be true. Generally speaking, Russians as a people tend to be less guarded about their emotional reactions; they can be said to act more spontaneously at times than one would expect. This—combined with the fact that some may have a few rough edges left by their backgrounds and life experiences—leads to the kind of behavior the world associates with Khrushchev at the United Nations, pounding the podium with his shoe to emphasize his point.

Consequently, almost nothing disarms and confuses a Russian more than a polite, carefully worded, but firm answer to his angry, sarcastic statement. The cultural expectation is that the other side will answer in kind. When that does not happen, he is forced in a way to reevaluate his opponent. Seeing the foreigner unruffled, politely smiling and firmly pursuing his argument, tends to make the Russian perceive new strength in his opponent.

There were a number of times that I perceived such group dynamics at our meetings. A university dean began to rant and rave about American youth having no appreciation for the difficulties still being encountered in Leningrad as a result of the long blockade during World War II. My colleague calmly and politely pointed out that all the students were required to read Harrison Salisbury's *900 Days* before their departure for the Soviet Union and that orientation for the program included discussions of the suffering and heroism of Leningradians during World War II. He added that American youth may be insensitive about some things, but not about Leningrad's history, and he was offended on their behalf that such a complaint would even be made. The calm, firm tone of my colleague clearly registered with those at the table; some even seemed visibly uncomfortable with the behavior of one of their own, who a few minutes before had charged the air with his angry accusations.

A few comments about the value of personal contact and interaction beyond the negotiating table are in order. Since any talks or discussions of any length will involve some socializing, be it over coffee and cognac or longer dinners at a restaurant, it is important to understand both the usefulness and limitations of such occasions.

It would be extremely naive and simpleminded to believe that a social affair or two, or even more, significantly changes a Soviet's attitude; but it would also be extremely shortsighted to think that dialogue in a more relaxed atmosphere has absolutely no effect on the individuals involved. Socializing—food, drink, casual conversation—allows individuals on both sides to relax a bit, to forget to some extent their official duties. It is no secret that Russians not only enjoy drinking, but often show a more humorous, friendly side after having shared a few toasts.

Of course, any remarks made under the influence of a few drinks and a more relaxed social atmosphere do not mean a change in negotiations the next day; but it is a fact that human interaction in a more relaxed atmosphere away from the talks table allows both sides to perceive each other on a more "human" level. Some of that tension brought about by the different socio-political convictions and experiences of both sides is at least temporarily removed. If the next day not much has changed in the way of expectations and tactics at the negotiating table, there still remains that imperceptible lingering effect of having been able to get to know each other just a little socially—to trade anecdotes, stories about families, life, etc. Positions on major and minor issues might not be affected, but it is a fact that it is more difficult for both sides to be cold and formal after drinking and laughing the day before together.

Moreover, it is only after Russians get to know you some-what more on the personal "human" level that they might venture to make a quiet suggestion during a break in the talks—be it in the corridor or at a social function. A few words might give you just the clue you need to understand why the Soviet side seems so immovable on a particular issue. Of course, a cynic might say that any hints from a Russian beyond the negotiating table are preprogrammed, just a clever ploy. My experience indicates that there are reasonable individuals everywhere who find themselves in the difficult position of not being able to speak openly at the negotiating table, yet who feel strongly enough to risk giving a few guarded hints to "the other side." One such individual we dealt with had always supported the program in the past. When he told us quietly, outside the meeting, that because of the political climate the Soviet side could not be persuaded to change its stance on an issue, we took his words to be sincere and appreciated his help.

After two weeks of talks in Leningrad and Moscow, we signed the protocol of agreement outlining in broad terms the services the Soviet side would provide and the financial and other obligations our side assumed in contracting for these services. We attended a farewell dinner in Moscow and practiced a ritual long part of any business (and social) dealings with the Russians: the exchange of gifts, souvenirs. The Russians have not forgotten the advice given in *The Russian Primary Chronicle* (11th century), which reads: " ... [M]ost of all honor your guest, wherever he may have come from, be he a peasant or a nobleman or an ambassador. If you cannot honor him with a gift, at least give him food and drink."

9

Citizen Diplomacy: One-Sided but Rewarding

Kurt M. Campbell

H EIGHTENED CONCERN in the United States about the deterioration in superpower relations and the specter of nuclear war has prompted Americans in ever greater numbers to travel to the Soviet Union on unofficial visits of goodwill. On my last visit to Moscow, I was surprised to meet members from no fewer than three other delegations who were touring the country and meeting with various Soviet organizations to express their concern over the failure of arms control.

More and more Americans, at the same time fascinated to see Russia firsthand and discouraged by the lack of dialogue between the United States and the USSR, are making the pilgrimage to the Soviet Union. Given the chill in relations between Moscow and Washington, the increase in "citizen diplomacy" is dramatic, but not without historical precedent.

Even before the United States accorded diplomatic recognition to the Soviet Union in 1933, some Americans were actively involved in trying to improve relations between the two countries. Armand Hammer journeyed to Russia shortly after the successful conclusion of the Bolshevik Revolution and, in addition to receiving a business concession from

This article is reprinted, by permission of the author, from the *Christian Science Monitor,* August 28, 1985.

Lenin himself, counseled the Soviet leaders that trade was the key to better relations with the West. Later, writers like John Gunther traveled around the Soviet Union and depicted in their works secrets of a country Stalin had succeeded in hiding from the world's view. Recent contacts between private citizens of the United States and the Soviet Union differ in several important respects from those instances:

- Earlier visitors were brought into contact with Russia largely as a result of their professions. Today's pilgrims have little or nothing to do with the Soviet Union professionally; their experience with Russia and Russians has been limited for the most part to what they have learned from the American news media.
- The propaganda value of these grass-roots visitors is often fully exploited by the Soviet government. The 1983 journey to the USSR of Maine schoolgirl Samantha Smith was carefully orchestrated by the Soviet propaganda apparatus to show Russia and Russians in the best possible light.
- Increased citizen diplomacy has served to raise hopes about again improving relations with Moscow. A recent visit by John Denver to Russia, which culminated in a "live" satellite television hookup between Moscow and San Francisco, was accorded unwarranted significance by some Western commentators. Perhaps the only meaningful "dialogue" resulting from this encounter was a zealous Russian interpreter's translation of John Denver's uplifting song, "Rocky Mountain High," as "Drunk in the Mountains."

Critics of these civilian encounters with the Soviet Union have attacked them as being naive, counterproductive, and even dangerous to diplomacy carried out through official channels. The detractors argue that while Western public opinion has helped to shape the arms-control agenda in the United States, there is no such thing as "public opinion" in the USSR. The elite who make Soviet foreign policy confer privately in the seclusion of the Kremlin, speed around Moscow in sleek black limousines, and shop in exclusive stores, isolated from their fellow Soviet citizens.

To date, there has been little reciprocity in these projects designed to bring Soviet and American people together. Americans have traveled to the Soviet Union by the score, but Soviet delegations to the United States continue to be composed primarily of senior officials. Indeed, the Soviet government has established, managed, and wholly controlled its "popular" peace movement from the start.

While there is merit in these criticisms, the process of citizen diplomacy should not be rejected out of hand. Instead, greater attention should be given to defining the objectives of unofficial contacts with the Soviet Union. Present and past attempts at civilian involvement in the complex affairs of state have suffered from a lack of appreciation of the differences between Soviet and American societies. Although we share a mutual interest in the avoidance of nuclear war, there are important cultural and political factors that serve to divide rather than unite us. A clear understanding of these differences should be foremost in the minds of those who seek to bridge the gap between our countries. In this respect, the educational value of such exchanges could be beneficial.

Perhaps the greatest contribution citizen diplomacy can make is in helping Americans understand both aspects of the dilemma. "Citizen diplomats" will come to see the ways the Soviets try to manipulate the situation for their own advantage. They will also discover that the Russian people, like Americans, have genuine aspirations for security and for a better life. Coming to realize both truths would probably be the most useful outcome of a trip to the Soviet Union.

10

Public Diplomacy and Other Exchanges

Yale Richmond

I N ADDITION TO high visibility and scholarly exchanges, a broad range of people-to-people exchanges with the Soviet Union has evolved over the past twenty-five years, some sponsored by the U.S. government, others by private institutions with government funding, and even more in recent years by the private sector with private funding. The common denominator in these efforts has been the face-to-face contact and dialogue they have facilitated between U.S. and Soviet citizens in a wide variety of professional fields. These activities, although centrally controlled and directed on the Soviet side, have made a positive contribution to the goal of freer exchanges of people, information, and ideas sought by all U.S. administrations.

Delegations and Seminars

Delegation exchanges have always been favored by the Soviets over individual exchanges. The delegation represents

This article is adapted from a study the author wrote for the Kennan Institute for Advanced Russian Studies, *Soviet-American Cultural Exchanges: Ripoff or Payoff?* (Washington: Woodrow Wilson International Center for Scholars, 1984). Reprinted by permission of the Wilson Center, Smithsonian Institution, Washington, DC.

what the Russians call a "kollektiv" (collective), which is a Russian as well as a Soviet tradition, but contrary to Western emphasis on the individual. And in a delegation the Soviet authorities have more possibilities for representing the various elements in their society—the republics, ethnics, government, party, and various "organs" such as the KGB.

Delegation exchanges were the rule between 1958 and 1972 when the main objective was to learn about the other country. Delegations were exchanged in all fields covered by the cultural agreement, from science and technology to culture and education. They ranged in size from five to ten or more, and usually visited for two weeks on study tours, being briefed on developments in their fields and getting an overview of the other country. On their return home delegations were debriefed, reports were written, and that was usually the end of the exchange. Follow-up was rare.

Seminars became popular during the détente years when both sides were seeking ways to broaden communication and cooperation. With détente there was also interest in moving to more substantive exchanges with continuity. Under the seminar format each side fields a delegation, and the two delegations meet for several days of in-depth discussion on a prearranged agenda, usually at an out-of-the-way retreat. This is followed—or preceded—by a study tour of about a week. There is usually some follow-up activity such as another seminar, some joint activity, and further exchanges.

The seminar is also attractive to the Soviets because with the two delegations sitting around a table, it implies equality between the two superpowers whose representatives meet as co-equals. The seminar also gives the Soviets a platform for promoting Soviet positions to a captive audience of prominent Americans.

The first U.S.-Soviet bilateral seminar was the Dartmouth Conference, a meeting of prominent Americans and Soviets held in 1960 at Dartmouth College under the leadership of Norman Cousins. [See chapters 2–4 above.—Ed.] The purpose of the Dartmouth Conference, Norman Cousins has said, was

> to identify areas of opportunity for both countries to reduce tension. Obviously, we relayed the results of each conference to

government. The conferences made it possible for both governments to try out certain ideas without penalty. . . . In this way a number of issues with respect to the test ban were aired very early. There is no doubt in my mind that the Dartmouth Conference had some part to play in the eventual treaty that came about.[1]

A similar series of conferences has been held by the U.S. United Nations Association (UNA) since 1969 under its Parallel Studies Program with the Soviet Union [discussed by Walter Stoessel in chapter 1—Ed.]. UNA conferences have focused on such issues as the environment, peaceful nuclear explosions, conventional arms control, North-South economic issues, and indebtedness in the Third World and Eastern Europe.

Soviet participants in both the Dartmouth and UNA conferences have come from the Soviet Academy of Sciences research institutes, from government ministries, the Party's Central Committee staff, the press, and more recently the Army General Staff. U.S. participants have included former cabinet members, directors of research institutions and major foundations, bankers, corporation heads, scholars and writers. The U.S. participants are all private citizens, although many have formerly served at high levels in the government, and they speak for themselves. The Soviets, by contrast, all represent and speak for the Soviet government.

Dartmouth and UNA have similar objectives—initiating discussion of topics not on the official negotiating agenda between the two governments, prodding the thinking of both governments on future issues, clarifying intentions, explaining sources of policy, exploring policy options, and gaining access to those who have inputs into foreign policy considerations.

The value of these conferences has been to provide a channel for private dialogue between the two countries, particularly when relations are not good, and indirect input to Soviet policymakers. The conferences have also been used by the Soviets to signal intentions and possible future moves in

---

[1]Maureen R. Berman and Joseph E. Johnson, *Unofficial Diplomats* (New York: Columbia University Press, 1977), p. 46.

arms control negotiations, the Middle East, bilateral trade, and economic and scientific cooperation.

Through these conferences the Soviets keep current on the views of a broad spectrum of U.S. political thought, including the administration as well as private groups both left and right of center. The conferences help the Soviets assess the future course of U.S. politics—what the next administration in Washington might do.

Critics point out that over the years the same faces tend to show up at these conferences, especially on the Soviet side, and an "old boys" network has developed. True, the Soviets often send the same people to meetings with Americans—those who have the confidence of the party, are experienced in debate with Americans and in presenting the Soviet viewpoint, and who speak English. A few people on each side have also provided the continuing leadership to keep the conferences going.

Georgiy Arbatov, Yuri Zhukov and other "old boys" are members of a select group of Soviets who are cleared for foreign travel, who very much enjoy this travel and regard it as one of the perks of having achieved status in the Soviet Union. Rank has its privilege in the Soviet Union too.

There is also a Russian reason why the Soviet "old boy" network persists in these and other meetings. In traditional Russian society—which still persists in the Soviet Union in many ways—older and more experienced people are believed to know best and should therefore represent their country abroad.

There are also sound arguments in defense of the "old boy" network. A good working relationship with the Soviets takes time to develop. Americans who have dealt with Soviets over the years know that the Soviets feel more comfortable in the company of familiar faces and show confidence and trust only after several meetings. In the Soviet Union, when something needs to be done, a citizen goes first, not to the person responsible, but to someone he knows who can perhaps help. Useful and productive discussions can be held between Americans and Soviets only after a good working relationship has been established. Thus, while efforts are made to bring new and younger people into these conferences, there are advantages to meeting repeatedly with some of the same people.

Patricia Derian commented on this aspect of U.S.-Soviet conferences after attending one in Minneapolis in June 1983 sponsored by the Institute for Policy Studies. The former assistant secretary of state for human rights in the Carter administration wrote: "The only way to comprehension is knowledge and experience. That won't come with meeting ten thousand Soviets or Americans once. It comes with meeting the same people over and over again, getting past opening statements and host/guest rituals to whatever else there is."[2]

Congressmen and Government Officials

Most high-level American political leaders have never visited the Soviet Union. Only 52 percent of U.S. senators had visited there as of January 1984, and the rate for House members is even less—28 percent—according to statistics kept current by the American Federation of Scientists.

For Soviet leaders the record is no better. Only twenty of one hundred leading Soviet officials had visited the United States by 1981, according to a study by Radio Liberty.[3]

To correct this, Senator Robert Dole offered a sense of the Senate resolution in July 1983 that "travel by members of the Senate to the Soviet Union serves the interests of the United States and should be, and is hereby, encouraged." A similar House resolution, offered by Representatives Paul Simon and Douglas Bereuter in February 1984, went one step further, endorsing travel by Soviet leaders to the United States as well as House members to the Soviet Union. Senator Mike Gravel in 1969 had introduced a bill that went even further, proposing to exchange one thousand U.S. elected officials and an equal number of Soviet officials over a five-year period, including

[2]*Washington Post,* June 9, 1983.
[3]*A Biographical Directory of 100 Leading Soviet Officials,* Radio Liberty Research Bulletin, Munich, February 10, 1981.

governors, mayors and state legislators, as well as congressmen.

Averell Harriman and George Kennan testified in support of the Gravel bill. One of our basic difficulties with the Soviet Union, said Harriman, is the lack of understanding of the United States on the part of Soviet officials because very few of them have travelled in the West. And lack of knowledge of the Soviet Union on the part of U.S. officials, added Harriman, has contributed to our difficulties.

It is reasonable to expect that members of Congress and high government officials should see the Soviet Union and talk with its leaders. The American officials make decisions affecting U.S.-Soviet relations, and the congressmen vote on foreign affairs and defense issues. They make "fact-finding" trips elsewhere; why not to the Soviet Union?

The Soviets sought exchanges between their Supreme Soviet and the U.S. Congress in the first cultural agreement, but the U.S. side was hesitant and it was agreed only to continue the discussions. It was not until 1962, under the third cultural agreement, that the two governments agreed to "render every assistance" to visiting members of the Congress and Supreme Soviet, as well as to officials of their national governments. In the same year there was also a new provision for exchanges between "municipal, local and regional governing bodies."

A number of U.S. senators and congressmen visited the Soviet Union in subsequent years, but it was not until 1974 that the first official exchange took place, when a Supreme Soviet delegation headed by Politburo member Boris Ponomarev visited the United States. A Senate delegation headed by Senators Humphrey and Scott made a return visit in 1975, and a House delegation headed by Speaker Carl Albert, in 1978. Another delegation exchange followed before the Soviet invasion of Afghanistan forced a halt.

Congress has been reluctant over the years to engage in formal exchanges with the Soviet Union. There is, first, the political sensitivity. Most congressmen don't win votes back home by going to the Soviet Union. There is also the time factor. These exchanges take congressmen from their other duties, and they open the door to similar exchanges with other countries. And some congressmen believe that formal exchanges with the Soviet Union equate the Congress to the Supreme Soviet and thereby give legitimacy to that body, which purports to represent the Soviet people. When high-level officials of the two countries exchange reciprocal visits, there is indeed an implied equivalency of position and stature, as well as legitimacy.

Chief Justice Warren Burger, for example, visited the Soviet Union during the summer of 1977 and invited his "counterpart," Chairman of the Soviet Supreme Court Lev Smirnov, to make a return visit to Washington. The position of the Soviet chief justice, however, is not equivalent in status to that of our chief justice, and Smirnov's visit to the United States gave the Soviet judicial system much more respectability than it deserves, particularly in view of the role it has played in the suppression of Soviet human rights.

Prior to détente there were few visits to either country by high-level government officials. In the 1970s, however, the annual meetings of the joint commissions to monitor the eleven bilateral cooperative agreements provided an opportunity for cabinet and subcabinet-level officials to exchange visits. These, too, ended with the invasion of Afghanistan and the decisions of the Carter and Reagan administrations to discourage high-level contacts.

During the détente years, there were also several exchanges of state governors and Soviet republic officials conducted by the National Governors Association, and exchanges of mayors by the U.S. Conference of Mayors. Both exchanges were suspended after 1979.

In summary, a start was made during the 1970s in exchanges of political and governmental leaders, but it was still far short of what the relationship between the two superpowers would call for.

Young Political Leaders

Young American political leaders have shown no hesitation in holding seminars with the Soviets. From 1971 to 1979, 165

Americans and 150 Soviets participated in meetings between young (forty and under) politicians on the rise in their countries' political structures. The exchange was suspended in 1980 after the invasion of Afghanistan.

The American Council of Young Political Leaders was the U.S. sponsor, representing young leaders of the Democratic and Republican parties. The Soviet sponsor was the USSR Committee of Youth Organizations, the government agency responsible for Komsomol, the Communist Party's youth division.

Most U.S. participants have been political leaders at the state and local levels, where political careers in the United States start. They have included state legislators, city council members, staffers of public and party officials, as well as lawyers, journalists, businessmen and trade union officials. The seminars in the Soviet Union were, for most of the Americans, their first visit to that country. More important, the five days spent in debate with the Soviets provided a unique opportunity to understand issues in U.S.-Soviet relations as seen from the Soviet as well as the American side, and the differences in culture, tradition, and history that separate the two countries.

Soviet participants have included Komsomol officials from the republic as well as the national level, party officials, editors and journalists, scholars from the Academy institutes, scientists, engineers and workers—groups from which the leaders of the Soviet Union have usually come. For most of them the seminars have provided their only opportunity to visit the United States.

What made these seminars different from the Dartmouth and UNA seminars is the relative youth on both sides and the inclination to speak more directly, and at times vociferously, without the diplomatic niceties and restraint that characterize the "older" seminars. Soviets appreciate straight talk from their adversaries. They got it from the young American political leaders and responded in kind. The two sixteen-person delegations were divided among four subcommittees, facilitating rapport and discussion, often on a one-on-one basis, as well as socializing during both day and evening sessions.

Funded in their first year by the Ford Foundation, these seminars in subsequent years were funded by the State Department and by USIA, 1978–79. They were interrupted by the Carter administration's suspension of cultural exchanges following the Soviet invasion of Afghanistan, and have remained suspended, despite several Soviet proposals to resume them, because of the Reagan administration's opposition to funding cultural exchanges with the Soviet Union.

Many U.S. participants have already reached positions of influence where their Soviet experience has been useful. These include three members of Congress, a state governor, lieutenant governor, state attorney general, chairman of the Republican National Committee, vice-chairman of the Democratic National Committee, chairman of the White House Domestic Policy Council, special assistant to the president, State Department spokesman, National Security Council staffer, university president, college president, syndicated columnist, editor of a newsletter, and corporation president.

On the Soviet side it is too early to see upward movement, given the priority that age has within the Soviet leadership. But because so many Komsomol leaders in the past have gone on to higher positions in the party and government, it can be assumed that many participants in these seminars will also.

One evidence of effectiveness of these seminars has been the change in the Soviet delegations' understanding of the United States and U.S.-Soviet bilateral issues. Soviet delegates to the first seminar in 1971 were almost totally ignorant about the United States. With their distorted view of history, they had limited ability to discuss Soviet-American issues and, as a consequence, were no match for the U.S. delegation. The seminars have forced the Soviets to field better delegations and to make sure that they were better informed about the realities of the United States and U.S.-Soviet relations.

U.S. views of the Soviet Union have also changed. As one American participant reported after a seminar in the Soviet Union, the conservatives in the U.S. delegation found they had more in common with the Soviets than they had anticipated, while the liberals discovered that they had less.

And More Public Diplomacy

Several new policy issue seminars have been held in recent years, sponsored by such diverse U.S. groups as the Institute for Policy Studies of Washington, D.C., and the Foreign Policy Research Institute of Philadelphia. Other U.S. sponsors of seminars with the Soviets include women's organizations, church groups, and peace activists. Their meetings with the Soviets, which have focused on arms control, security, and peace issues, are evidence of a public concern that the U.S. government has not been doing enough on these issues and that dialogue with the Soviets should be broadened through public diplomacy. In this regard, it is ironic that the Reagan administration, by continuing the Carter administration's suspension of cultural exchanges, has left the field wide open to citizen groups, many of which are opposed to its policies on the Soviet Union.

U.S. public dialogue with the Soviet Union needs to be broadened and the participation of all groups should be welcomed. U.S. citizen groups, however, should understand with whom they are meeting. The Soviets, in their meetings with U.S. citizen groups, staff their delegations with experienced and skilled propagandists who are veterans of the Soviet "peace" movement and who represent the Soviet government and communist party. They are often not in the same league with the visiting Americans.

The Americans in these meetings speak only for themselves, but they bear a responsibility in also representing the United States. This does not mean they should necessarily defend the administration's policies. Rather, they should try to help the Soviets to understand the U.S. political process, the wide range of public opinion on various issues, and how these views are ultimately presented, through elections, to the White House and the Congress. Above all, the Americans should avoid being exploited by the Soviets for political purposes. Public diplomacy can do some good in U.S.-Soviet relations, but it can also cause some damage.

Llewellyn Thompson, one of our most astute observers of the Soviet Union, commented on the hazards of dealing with

the Soviet Union. In his final meeting with American corre-
spondents in Moscow, just prior to leaving after completing
his second tour there as U.S. ambassador, Thompson was
asked what he regarded as his greatest accomplishment. "That
I didn't make things any worse," he replied.

Other Exchanges

There are many other exchanges that don't make the headlines—small Soviet delegations or individual visits in such
fields as culture, education, journalism, and politics—in response to invitations from the U.S. government and private
organizations. During the 1970s many Soviets came under the
State Department's (now USIA's) International Visitor Program for up to thirty-day visits. In exchange, the Soviets have
permitted the U.S. embassy in Moscow to bring in American
speakers on a broad range of subjects, under USIA's American Participant Program, to meet with and address Soviet
groups.

Trips abroad for Soviet citizens, it has been charged, are
payoffs for party loyalty and ideological orthodoxy. This is
certainly true in many cases, and the practice is not unknown
in other countries, including our own. But among those
Soviets who have come to the United States are such inter-
nationally respected figures as the composers Dmitri Sho-
stakovich, Dmitri Kabalevsky, and Rodion Shchedrin; poets
Andrei Voznesensky and Yevgeny Yevtushenko; theater directors Oleg Yefremov, Anatoly Efros, and Galina Volchek;
writers Valentin Katayev, Yuri Trifonov, Chengiz Aitmatov,
Vitaliy Korotich, and Vladimir Soloukhin; and playwright
Mikhail Roshchin. To get persons of this caliber, the United
States has had to accept some of the others as well.

11

Psychological Principles of Citizen Diplomacy

James L. Hickman
James A. Garrison, Jr.

I N THE FIELD of Soviet-American relations, something dramatic and new is happening. For the first time, numerous private citizens and organizations have begun to incorporate international diplomacy into their sense of personal responsibility. They have become diplomats, but not in a way that undercuts government diplomacy. Citizen diplomacy is meant to complement government diplomacy; its objective is to create a supportive structure for government action.

Joseph Montville, a career diplomat who is currently research director of the Center for the Study of Foreign Affairs at the U.S. State Department's Foreign Service Institute, coined the term "track two" diplomacy to designate citizen initiatives between nations. Track two refers to constructive, unofficial, informal interactions between individuals and groups on different sides of ethnic and sectarian conflicts. Conceived as an adjunct to track one diplomacy (official, traditional, nation-to-nation channels), track two seeks to reduce psychological barriers between contending parties, creating new possibilities for negotiation on more formal levels.

Montville points out that political leaders are like tribal chiefs in that they must assure their followers they will defend them against competitors. Even the most sophisticated leaders must adopt forceful postures at crucial moments to meet this most primitive but enduring need of people living in groups. The problem is that this necessary and predictable leadership function often draws groups into conflicts. Concrete political or economic grievances, compounded by historical and cultural factors, often lead to misperception and thus to lost opportunities to resolve differences before the fighting begins. A second diplomatic track can therefore make its contribution as a supplement to the understandable limitations of official relations, especially in times of tension. If it is the role of leaders to defend, it can be the useful role of certain citizens to extend a hand in friendship.

Track two diplomacy, because of its unofficial, nonstructured interactions, can afford to be "strategically optimistic," to use the words of Harvard social psychologist Herbert C. Kelman. Its underlying assumption is that actual or potential conflicts can be resolved or eased by appealing to common human capabilities to respond to good will and imagination. What needs to be underscored, says Montville, is that "reasonable and altruistic interaction with foreign countries cannot be an alternative to traditional track one diplomacy, with its official posturing and its underlying threat of the use of force. Both tracks are necessary for psychological reasons and both need each other." In fact, he adds, "people may respond more readily to track two diplomacy if they are first reassured that their leaders will defend their interests."*

Sending private emissaries either overtly or covertly to foreign lands has been a recognized and accepted tool of diplomacy for perhaps as long as there has been diplomacy. It has been essential to the conduct of diplomacy during the Cold War, as when President Eisenhower, feeling blocked at the level of government-to-government communication, sent Norman Cousins to discuss with Nikita Khrushchev what private citizens representing a broad range of American public opinion could do to help ease the tension between the

*William D. Davidson and Joseph V. Montville, "Foreign Policy According to Freud," in *Foreign Policy* 45 (Winter 1981–82):145–57.

two superpowers [as described by Philip Stewart in chapter 2—Ed.].

Several considerations led Cousins to believe that unofficial, informal, and private gatherings would be an effective way to build personal rapport across ideologies. Official negotiations, mainly on disarmament, had yielded little in the way of substantive agreements. Perhaps even more important to Cousins was his belief that in the nuclear age the vital questions of the future of humanity were too important to leave to governments. Private citizens, he believed, should seek to contribute in a responsible way to the dialogues between nations on issues of peace and security.

The timing for such a suggestion was right: In 1958, a cultural exchange agreement had been signed by Eisenhower and Khrushchev, and Khrushchev quickly agreed that the Soviet Peace Committee would take up Cousins' proposal under this larger agreement. The resulting Dartmouth Conferences constitute the oldest continuing exercise in bilateral communication between Soviet and American citizens since the Second World War.

Individuals have also been called upon to help mediate crises. In 1978, President Carter called upon Dr. Olin Robison, president of Middlebury College, to help negotiate the exchange of two American-held Soviet spies and five Soviet dissidents. This exchange marked the first time an American negotiator traded Soviets for Soviets. Robison's success in this exchange laid the basis for another task: securing a negotiated settlement for the families of seven Soviet Pentacostalists who had taken refuge in the American embassy in Moscow. Robinson negotiated with the Soviets on behalf of President Carter and then on behalf of President Reagan. In 1983, a resolution was obtained: the Pentacostalists left the embassy and went home, as required by the Soviet government. They were then given the exit visas they had gone to the embassy to obtain in the first place.

The New Citizen Diplomats

The burst of citizen diplomacy since 1980 builds on what has gone before. It has been similarly motivated by the inability of government to deal creatively with major problems, such as the Cold War, and has been made possible through the accessibility of the American government to its citizens and their freedom to travel to the Soviet Union.

At the same time, what has been happening is unique, because recent citizen diplomacy is not limiting itself merely to supporting or mediating government policies. Citizen diplomats from America have been setting their own agendas, careful not to antagonize the governments but nevertheless certain that they have a responsibility to create their own relationships and momentums with the Soviets, to which the governments can then respond rather than dictate.

What is particularly innovative about these citizen diplomats is that their activities cover the whole spectrum of issues and concerns. Esalen Institute's Soviet-American Exchange Program, for instance, evolved out of the human potential movement. Contacts with like-minded colleagues in the Soviet Union generated numerous contacts, initially in the fields of psychical research and exceptional human performance, but then increasingly in areas as diverse as astronaut-cosmonaut dialogues, health promotion, satellite communication, entertainment, and the political psychology of Soviet-American relations.

The Institute for Soviet-American Relations (ISAR), based in Washington, D.C., grew out of Esalen's initiatives. Its first project was to catalogue the U.S. organizations that are engaged in citizen diplomacy and related public education activities, some two hundred in 1983, an astounding number given the fact that there were fewer than half a dozen organizations so involved at the end of World War II. These findings were published in 1983 in a handbook entitled, *Organizations Involved in Soviet-American Relations* (updated in 1986). Subsequently, ISAR produced another handbook, *Inviting and Sponsoring Soviet Guests.* ISAR also publishes *Surviving Together,* a newsletter reporting the latest activities of citizen diplomats and analyzing the issues arising from such activities.

Several other organizations exemplify the breadth of the current wave of citizen-diplomacy activity. The U.S.-Soviet Youth Exchange, a San Francisco–based organization, has designed and successfully field-tested learning resource packets about the Soviet Union for use in schools, churches, and community organizations. Using videotapes, color slides, and essays written by Soviet students, the lessons emphasize cross-cultural contrast and comparison between Soviet and American cultures. For the past two summers, the Youth Exchange has sponsored a wilderness adventure trek in the Caucasus Mountains for young Soviets and Americans. On the other end of the spectrum is Ark Communications of Bolinas, California, which seeks to resolve international conflict through the application of advanced communication technologies. One of its major endeavors has been to link Soviet and American scientists through computer conferencing.

There are also organizations like the Harvard Negotiation Project and the Nuclear Negotiating Project [NNP] directed by Professor Roger Fisher and Dr. William Ury respectively. The Harvard Negotiation Project is concerned with improving the theory and practice of negotiation, especially in legal and international contexts. A major focus of the project is on U.S.-Soviet negotiations and the U.S.-Soviet relationship. The Nuclear Negotiation Project explores how negotiation can reduce the risk of nuclear war. The NNP's report to the U.S. government, *Beyond the Hotline,* proposed six concrete measures for preventing and controlling a nuclear crisis, including a U.S.-Soviet crisis control center. The project is developing these measures further and investigating their feasibility with both American and Soviet specialists and officials.

The Changing Context

These activities are all happening in the midst of tremendous changes in the American public's perceptions of nuclear war and attitudes toward the Soviet Union. Americans no longer believe, as they once did, that nuclear war is winnable and survivable. In 1955, a Gallup poll found that only a quarter of the public (27 percent) agreed that "mankind would be destroyed in an all-out atomic or hydrogen bomb war." By 1961, a larger minority (43 percent) had come to believe they would have a poor chance of surviving such a war. In 1984, a two-thirds majority (68 percent) held this view regardless of the question's wording.

In part, this change reflects Americans' revised understanding of the relative strengths of the United States and the Soviet Union. When the United States alone had the bomb, most Americans had few doubts about our safety. After the Soviets achieved nuclear status, and even after they had developed the hydrogen bomb, Americans' confidence in their nuclear superiority still provided a feeling of security. Today, only 10 percent of Americans believe America has nuclear superiority; a majority now feel that the two sides are roughly equal in destructive capability—at a level felt to be terrifying.

There have been subtle but far-reaching changes in Americans' thinking about communism as well. Beyond the McCarthy period and well into the sixties, Americans expressed fear that communism might spread, not only in this country but also among our allies in Europe. Communism was viewed as a monolithic ideology that threatened freedom everywhere.

Today, Americans have reached a position on communism that can best be described as pragmatic rejection. As they have in the past, Americans firmly reject the values of communism and see them as opposed to everything America stands for. But there is little fear today that communist subversion threatens the United States. In fact, a Public Agenda survey in 1984 showed that an overwhelming majority of the public concurred that "our experience with communist China proves that our mortal enemies can quickly turn into countries we can get along with" (83 perecnt). The belief that communism is something Americans can tolerate without endorsing represents another, perhaps fundamental, shift in the public's thinking since the beginning of the nuclear age.

What the polls seem to indicate about American perceptions of the Soviets is that although our two political cultures represent fundamentally different value systems, war is simply not an option for settling our differences. Nuclear weapons are forcing us to begin to live with our disappointments in one another.

Psychological Principles of Citizen Diplomacy

The initiatives of citizen diplomacy are directly linked to the psychology of the nuclear era that compels us to explore creative solutions in the midst of traditional antagonisms. It is the challenge of citizen diplomacy to change the symbiotic relationship between the leader and the led by seeing international relations as an area where personal initiative can bring positive results. By engaging Soviets and Americans in endeavors that bring them together as equals, in a way that benefits both sides, citizen diplomacy can create the type of psychological context in which governments can be empowered to define national security as both a defense and an integration of national interests.

This does not mean that citizen diplomacy emphasizes only aspects of commonality between Soviets and Americans and ignores the differences. On the contrary. In dealing with the Soviet people, it is important to understand that although Americans and Soviets share a common humanity at one level, fundamental differences divide us at another. Unless we can appreciate both our commonality and our differences, Americans cannot hope to develop successful relations with the Soviets.

A major difference in our societies is described by anthropologist Edward Hall, who divides cultures into high context and low context types. Americans are a very low context society. What is being said is more important than the larger context in which the message is being sent and received. Americans emphasize specificity of content, and because they are relatively unconcerned about context, they value the qualities of honesty, flexibility, and initiative. When confronted by a complex problem, Americans tend to break it down into its component parts.

The Soviet Union, on the other hand, is a very high context culture. For Soviets, the setting in which a message is sent and received is as important as the message. If Americans stress content, Soviets stress context. If Americans seek to break complex problems down, Soviets tend to emphasize the general setting out of which complex problems emerge. It is nearly impossible to talk about a contemporary political issue with a Soviet official without the official at some point mentioning the heavy Soviet losses during World War II. Soviets go for the big picture. They emphasize the general over the particular, the sweep of history over the immediate political concerns. The Soviets know how to wait, something foreign to Americans, whose political economy is predicated on taking the waiting out of wanting.

Psychologist Steven Kull offers the images of a motorboat and a sailboat to explore the differences between how Americans and Soviets view themselves. Americans are like motorboats. They are inwardly motivated and emphasize their uniqueness and individuality. They assume that they are acting in an autonomous, inner-directed way, independent of external forces. They therefore tend to emphasize personal initiative and creativity over conformity and cooperation. For Americans, truth is an absolute perspective that they arrive at individually. They value one-to-one loyalties above group loyalties. For Americans, the bigger the entity, the less their allegiance to it.

Soviets, on the other hand, are more like sailboats. Their system is such that rather than being inner-directed, they are compelled to be more aware of the environment—metaphorically, the wind and the movements of the sea. They stress the situation they are in as the causal factor in their behavior. For them, truth is derived more from social consensus than from an inward process; group loyalty is preeminent, especially when dealing with foreigners. The major exceptions to this are the Soviet dissidents, who personify the age-old Russian tradition of courageous individuality in the face of centralized control.

The above statements are, of course, rough generalizations.

No culture is exclusively high or low context. Yet for citizen diplomats working with Soviet citizens, the observations by Edward Hall and Steven Kull have proven useful. They have learned to be sensitive to the Soviets' perspective on their own culture and on the foreign influences on their society. It is a very different perspective from that of the Americans. It is made up of very different values about personal freedom, political rights, and social organization.

To empathize with the Soviet perspective, however, requires high self-esteem, a highly developed sense of personal identity, and a high degree of individual security on the part of the citizen diplomat. With these psychological traits, one is able, even if briefly, to relinquish one's own point of view and see the world through Soviet eyes, secure in the knowledge that this perspective will neither deny nor destroy one's own values. There will always be points where they do not and cannot join. Successful citizen diplomats have been careful not to err, as many American liberals do, by overemphasizing cultural similarities and denying differences, or as many conservatives do, by overemphasizing the differences and denying the similarities. They have discovered that somewhere in the middle lies the ground where Soviets and Americans can come together to meet their long-term mutual objectives without destroying their independent integrities.

This attitude requires a balance between knowing when to yield and knowing when to be firm. The Soviets respect strength and are often disposed to pushing and taking when there is no resistance. Yet if there is a firmness about one's boundaries, about one's self-esteem and discipline, they can respond creatively in ways that are of mutual benefit.

It is important, therefore, for Americans to be Americans, to embody those ideals that have characterized this country for several centuries, namely, freedom and equality—ideals no other country has enjoyed in such bounty. With the Soviets in particular, Americans must not get caught in the spy game, which is to deny who they are, but must maintain a posture of honesty, openness, and personal security that creates opportunities for new types of interactions. Being an American is not about having enough weapons to destroy the world, but about a way of being in the world that embodies certain human ideals.

At the same time, Americans must allow the Soviets to be who *they* are. The worst mistake some liberals make is to project onto the Soviets the American liberal ideal, believing that if we are nice and open with them, the Soviets will change their system to a closer approximation of the American dream. Inevitably, this liberal expectation is disappointed, perhaps most poignantly expressed in President Carter's surprised disbelief that the Soviets had really invaded Afghanistan. The immediate response is to charge the Soviets with deception (something Carter did) and to feel betrayed. But what is being betrayed is only the liberal projection of what the Soviets should be; in fact, the Soviets have never embraced the American liberal tradition. Brezhnev was dumbfounded that Carter could not understand the Soviet imperative to enter Afghanistan. It is perhaps because of a widespread failure to allow the Soviets to be Soviet that most American Sovietologists find the object of their study distasteful.

Nuclear age diplomacy requires the ability to hold two points of view simultaneously. It requires an ability to comprehend the other point of reference in a way that enriches one's own ability to deal with that other point of view. This means developing a tolerance for ambiguity that understands both the significant differences that divide Soviets from Americans and the profound similarities that unite Soviets with Americans.

A fundamental component of citizen diplomacy, then, is the need to understand one's own psychology, in terms of not only how one is affected by the outside world but also how one projects one's inner emotional state and political ideals onto others. Though at first glance it may seem trivial, a compelling example of this occurred several years ago when Esalen sponsored Elmer and Alye Green's travel to the Soviet Union. The Greens lectured at various research institutes and conducted training programs in biofeedback and stress management for members of the Soviet health care community and for senior staff at the U.S. embassy. After receiving the training, one of the senior attachés told the Greens that he had discovered something very important about the way he interpreted intelligence data and made decisions. Part of his task at the embassy was to analyze information from a variety of sources. The biofeedback training allowed him to see that certain types of information, particularly about Soviet repression of scientists and dissidents, caused tension in his stomach. He realized that when his emotional response was one of tension, he tended to interpret the data differently than when he was relaxed.

What can be learned from this is that there is more to all of us than the prevailing dominant paradigm of scientific rationalism would indicate. Cognitive thought is not the only way humans interpret and experience reality. Information comes to us from a diversity of sources and is registered at a variety of levels. It is the ability to listen at all levels that is critical for selecting the appropriate response. Body language, nonverbal communication, emotional states during information transactions—all must be assimilated if one is to act with sensitivity. Using only an intellectual basis for decision making leads to prejudice, because it is not based on psychological grounding. Citizen diplomats are discovering that the deeper one's personal psychological integration, the more effectively one can operate politically.

Expanding Opportunities for Creative Interaction

It is this commitment on the part of citizen diplomats—both to empathize with the Soviet perspective and to consider the emotional and psychological components of human relationships—that has allowed them to approach the Soviets in new areas and in new ways. Citizen diplomats do not fit the traditional mold; therefore, they cannot be handled in traditional ways by the various Soviet organizations with which they deal.

Conversely, because of their established presence in Moscow, organizations such as the Academy of Sciences and the

State Committee on Radio and Television (Gosteleradio) have had to adapt to the variety of projects that have emerged from citizen diplomacy. In the beginning, the Soviets found it difficult to deal with the number of citizen diplomats, but have since responded to the efforts quite inventively. The first formal evidence of this appeared in early 1984 when, for the first time, the Soviets appointed a third secretary at their embassy in Washington just to deal with nongovernmental American initiatives.

The more creative citizen diplomats have worked with their Soviet counterparts to find new ways of collaborating with established professional organizations such as the Academy of Sciences, Gosteleradio, the Ministry of Culture, and others. Creative citizen diplomacy can help encourage Soviet willingness to allow foreign groups to develop constructive ties with their country. It also enables Americans to experience extraordinarily creative Soviet people and organizations that want sustained contact.

Citizen diplomats have discovered that the Soviet Union is a rich, complex, and multifaceted society. It is a system that is rigid, compartmentalized, and bureaucratic. It is also a system in which there is significant room for movement and change, though at a pace and in a direction very different from that of the United States. There are individuals who work within the Soviet system, developing permissible ways to bring new creativity into their culture. Citizen diplomats are directing their attention toward an alliance with these Soviets to identify informed policy directions in which both sides can work together.

A key element of this work for citizen diplomats, then, is having Soviet friends and allies who are both well informed about their system and committed to the vision of linking the two countries in some substantial way. With such contacts, preliminary discussions about project ideas can be organized to determine how to achieve agreed objectives within the constraints of both systems. It has been important to work in the Soviet Union without violating their laws, their cultural values, or the personal boundaries they observe.

The task for citizen diplomats has been to refrain from putting an American cultural overlay on the Soviet bureaucratic system. Citizen diplomats have been willing to be educated by Soviets about how to deal with the Soviet system in a more constructive way. The goal has been to actualize a vision of human beings working together to move both systems forward creatively.

A common Soviet maxim is that "anything that is not strictly prohibited is permitted." The challenge is to know enough about the system to understand what is prohibited and what is not, then to take action appropriate to the development of a new, less constraining governing rule. The use of rock music at the first satellite link-up, for example, meant that rock music in satellite link-ups ultimately might not be prohibited.

Many citizen diplomats have benefited from designing projects that involve the participation of more than one ministry. Esalen, for instance, is multidisciplinary and involves American specialists from a variety of disciplines and professions. Its programs in the Soviet Union are of interest to many Soviet ministries, institutes and organizations. In April of 1984, for example, Esalen signed a protocol with the Soviet Ministry of Printing, Publishing and Book Trade (Goskomizdat) that called for reciprocal book exhibitions in both our countries on health promotion. In January and February of 1985, one thousand American books covering areas such as stress, sports and physical fitness, child care, alternative therapies, psychology, and death and dying were exhibited at the National Library of Medical Sciences in Moscow and the National Library of Science and Technology in Novosibirsk. The ministers of publishing and health attended the opening of the Moscow exhibition. Accompanying the books was an American delegation that included Myrin Borysenko, Ph.D., research immunologist at Tufts University School of Medicine; John Mack, M.D., psychiatrist at Harvard Medical School; Sally Mack, M.A., specialist in parent-child bonding; and Joan Ullyot, M.D., specialist in sports medicine. Both exhibitions were well attended by the Soviet public and enjoyed widespread coverage by Soviet media. Members of the delegation gave lectures and took part in seminars in their fields of expertise.

In April 1985, the Soviets reciprocated by sending a seven-member delegation to California with one thousand Soviet books in the medical sciences and health fields. The books were exhibited at the UCLA School of Nursing and the Fort Mason Center in San Francisco. The delegates, three of whom were in the United States under the auspices of *Scientific American*, followed a full schedule of meetings, lectures, press interviews, and entertainment. They represented the Ministry of Publishing, Mir Publishers, the National Research Center on Psychoneuroendocrinology, the Vishnevsky Institute of Surgery, and the National Research Center for Lung Surgery.

These reciprocal exhibitions underscored the fact that both our societies are plagued by essentially the same major health problems: cancer, heart failure, and stress. The mutual exchanges brought out how differently each society is coping with these problems and therefore how much we can learn from one another. During the Soviet visit, Esalen developed another protocol, this one with the Soviet Ministry of Health, to continue collaboration through an ongoing series of exchanges and a joint monograph on stress, health, and disease.

This combination of empathizing with Soviets without denying one's American loyalties, acknowledging the psychological and emotional components of decision making, working with Soviets within the constraints of their own system, and developing innovative projects with various ministries and organizations is fundamental to successful citizen diplomacy. It is important to stress, however, that these observations are not being made from a position of fixed authority. They are only a first summary of the guiding principles emerging from experience, which are just beginning to be examined in a systematic way. They are put forward more to promote discussion than to pronounce final judgment.

Citizen diplomats have tried to move from confrontation to cooperation, believing that the historic differences and antagonisms between the Soviet and American peoples can be placed on a new footing—one that seeks to discover areas of potential collaboration, while appreciating real differences.

The steps taken by citizen diplomacy have been tentative, albeit exciting and rewarding. There is a high casualty rate for individuals working in the field of Soviet-American relations. Experience in this field can lead to disillusionment. When Soviets and Americans meet each other, there will be an extraordinary amount of creative tension. There will be guilt, there will be dreams, there will be suspicion. Above all, perhaps, there will be hope. Our mutual antagonisms must be dealt with while we experience the excitement of discovering new emotions in and with each other.

About the Authors

LANDRUM R. BOLLING, president of the Inter-Faith Academy of Peace, is an experienced practitioner of nonofficial diplomacy in Middle East initiatives, the Dartmouth Conference, and elsewhere. A former war correspondent and political science professor, he was president of Earlham College, 1958–73, the Lilly Foundation, 1973–75, and the Council on Foundations, 1975–78. As research professor of diplomacy at Georgetown University's Institute for the Study of Diplomacy, 1981–83, he edited the book *Reporters Under Fire: U.S. Media Coverage of Conflicts in Lebanon and Central America* (1985). Earlier publications included *This Is Germany* (coauthor, 1950), *Search for Peace in the Middle East* (1970), and *Private Foreign Aid: U.S. Philanthropy in Relief and Development* (coauthor, 1982). Dr. Bolling has an A.B. from the University of Tennessee, an A.M. from the University of Chicago, and over twenty-five honorary doctorates from U.S. and foreign universities.

VALENTINA GOLONDZOWSKI BROUGHER is assistant professor and chairman of Russian at Georgetown University. In 1983 she was resident director of the Russian Language Study Program at Leningrad State University, a program sponsored by the Council on International Educational Exchange [CIEE]. On previous trips to the Soviet Union, Professor Brougher was one of two negotiators for this CIEE Program (1979) and, earlier, group leader for the program (1968, 1971, and 1974). She has translated stories by several contemporary

Russian writers, including V. Rasputin, V. Aksenov, and S. Zalygin. She has presented papers and published book reviews and articles on Russian language study programs and Russian literature in the *Russian Language Journal, Canadian Slavonic Papers, Slavic and East European Journal,* and *Georgetown Magazine.* She holds a B.A. from Bryn Mawr College, an M.A. in Russian literature from Columbia University, and a Ph.D. in Slavic languages and literature from the University of Kansas.

KURT M. CAMPBELL has been Olin Fellow at the Russian Research Center, Harvard University, since 1985. In 1978–79, on a grant from the Soviet government, he studied Soviet politics, Russian literature, and performance violin at the University of Erevan in Soviet Socialist Armenia, where he was a member of the Soviet State Tennis Team. He holds a B.A. from the University of California, San Diego, and a Ph.D. from Oxford University, where he was a Marshall scholar and a graduate fellow. Dr. Campbell has presented papers and published articles on Soviet policy in southern Africa, the Soviet Union and the North-South dialogue, and aspects of international development. In 1983–84, he was a research associate at the International Institute for Strategic Studies in London.

JAMES AMON GARRISON, JR. is director of the Esalen Institute Soviet-American Exchange Program, a citizen diplomacy project. He was codirector and cofounder of East-West Reach (1983–85), which organized similar activities with the Soviet Union in Britain and Western Europe. Dr. Garrison has coauthored a number of publications, including *The Russian Threat: Its Myth and Realities* (1985), *Citizen Diplomacy: Taking Personal Responsibility for International Relations* (1986), and a chapter in *Citizen Summitry* (1986). An active opponent of nuclear power, he cofounded and codirected the Radiation and Health Information Service in Cambridge, England (1979–83). He received his B.A. from the University of Santa Clara, an M.T.S. from Harvard University Divinity School, and a Ph.D. from Cambridge University.

ARMAND HAMMER is chairman of the board and chief executive officer of Occidental Petroleum and president of Hammer Galleries. His varied occupations have ranged from doctor, entrepreneur, industrialist, and art dealer to oilwell driller, cattle breeder, and philanthropist. He first became involved in private negotiations with Soviet heads of state when he founded the Armand Hammer Pencil Co. in Moscow in 1925. He received his B.S. and M.D. degrees from Columbia University and honorary doctorates from various U.S. and foreign institutions. Among his other honors and prizes is the Order of Friendship among Peoples, received from the Soviet Union in 1978. Dr. Hammer is a board member of the U.S.-U.S.S.R. Trade and Economic Council, is actively involved in numerous civic, cultural, and philanthropic activities, and has endowed, among others, the Harvard/Columbia Russian Study Fund.

JAMES L. HICKMAN, a founder of the Esalen Institute Soviet-American Exchange Program in San Francisco, is a research psychologist specializing in political psychology, human development, and communications. As a consultant to U.S. corporations and educational institutions, he organizes and coordinates projects between American and Soviet academics and professionals. His projects have included the first live US–USSR interactive television transmission; dialogues between astronauts and cosmonauts; an exchange of U.S. and Soviet writers; simulation games on U.S. and Soviet decision-making processes; and studies of psychological dimensions of the U.S.-Soviet political relationship. As president of Sunsight Productions, he coordinates Soviet-American entertainment and educational projects, such as films and concert tours.

JEANNE VAUGHN MATTISON is cofounder of East-West Issues, a Washington-based research and consulting firm. From 1977 to 1985, she was codirector and director of the American Committee on East-West Accord. In that capacity, she wrote and produced an award-winning documentary, "Survival or Suicide" (1979), and initiated the "Ambassadors Emeriti" program of high-level private meetings between U.S. and

Soviet foreign policymakers, including seven former U.S. ambassadors to Moscow. Ms. Mattison has also held executive positions in several other public interest organizations, including the Council on Economic Priorities and the Coalition on National Priorities and Military Policy (1969–71); the Federation of American Scientists (1972–73); and the Council for a Livable World (1973–77).

DAVID D. NEWSOM is director of the Institute for the Study of Diplomacy and associate dean of the School of Foreign Service at Georgetown University. A career diplomat, he served as U.S. under secretary of state for political affairs from 1978 to 1981, was ambassador to the Philippines (1977–78), ambassador to Indonesia (1974–77), assistant secretary of state for African Affairs (1969–74), and ambassador to Libya (1965–69). He is president of the American Academy of Diplomacy and a board member of numerous international affairs organizations. Ambassador Newsom was editor of *The Diplomacy of Human Rights* (1986) and is a frequent contributor to foreign policy journals and the *Christian Science Monitor*. He has a B.A. degree from the University of California, Berkeley, and an M.S. from the Columbia University School of Journalism.

YALE RICHMOND is program officer for the Soviet Union and Eastern Europe at the National Endowment for Democracy. He is the author of *U.S.-Soviet Cultural Exchanges: Who Wins?* (1986), based on his 1984 monograph for the Kennan Institute for Advanced Russian Studies. In 1980–84, he was consultant to the U.S. Commission on Security and Cooperation in Europe, monitoring aspects of the Helsinki Accords. His lengthy service with the U.S. Information Agency and Department of State has included posts in Germany, Vientiane, Warsaw, Vienna, and Moscow. He was deputy assistant director (Europe) for the U.S. International Communication Agency (1978–79) and State Department director and deputy director of Soviet and East European Exchanges and International Visitor Programs (1971–78). Mr. Richmond has a B.S.

from Boston College, a B.E.E. from Syracuse University, and an M.A. from Columbia University.

HAROLD H. SAUNDERS, a resident fellow at the American Enterprise Institute, participated in the mediation of five Arab-Israeli agreements during the 1973–79 peace process. He accompanied Secretary of State Kissinger on his "shuttle diplomacy" missions and worked with President Carter and Secretary of State Vance at Camp David in negotiating the Egyptian-Israeli peace treaty. Since 1981, he has cochaired a Dartmouth Conference task force on Soviet-U.S. relations in areas of regional conflict and has participated in a number of private dialogues between Israelis and Arabs. During the previous twenty years, he was assistant secretary of state for Near Eastern and South Asian affairs (1978–81) and deputy assistant secretary (1974–75); director of State Department intelligence and research (1975–78); and a National Security Council staff member (1961–74).

ROBERT D. SCHMIDT is president of MinneAspen Associates, a management consulting firm, and chairman of the American Committee on U.S.-Soviet Relations (formerly American Committee on East-West Accord). He was chief executive officer and chairman of Earth Energy Systems, Inc. (1983–85). From 1962 to 1983, he held a wide range of management and policy positions at Control Data Corporation. Mr. Schmidt has been chairman, director, vice chairman, or board member of numerous corporate and professional organizations, including the Computer and Business Equipment Manufacturers Association, the President's Export Council, and the Department of Commerce East-West Advisory Committee. He has authored journal articles and a chapter in *A Game of High Stakes: Lessons Learned in Negotiating with the Soviet Union* (1986). He holds a B.A. from Mankato State College and pursued graduate studies at Oklahoma, George Washington and Northeastern universities.

PHILIP D. STEWART is professor of political science and director of the Program in Soviet International Behavior at Ohio State University. He has been rapporteur with the Dartmouth Conference since 1972, a participant since 1980, and coordinator since 1981. He is the author of *Political Power in the Soviet Union: A Study of Decision Making in Stalingrad* (1968) and two forthcoming works, on Soviet foreign policy perspectives from Brezhnev to Gorbachev and on Soviet leadership and economic change in the 1970s. His numerous journal articles include "Gorbachev and Obstacles toward Détente" in *Political Science Quarterly* (January 1986). He holds a B.A. from Northwestern University, M.A. and Ph.D. degrees from Indiana University, and was an exchange student at Moscow State University in 1962–63.

WALTER J. STOESSEL, JR., a career diplomat from 1942 to 1982, was U.S. ambassador to Poland in 1968–72, ambassador to the Soviet Union, 1974–76, and ambassador to the Federal Republic of Germany, 1976–81. He was deputy assistant secretary of state for European Affairs (1965–68), later assistant secretary (1972–74). Ambassador Stoessel served as under secretary of state for political affairs in 1981, then as deputy secretary of state until his retirement in 1982. Earlier, he studied Russian and served as officer in charge of U.S.S.R. affairs in the State Department and later (1963) as deputy chief of mission in Moscow. He also served as deputy director, then director of the State Department executive secretariat and as counselor at Supreme Headquarters in Paris (SHAPE). He attended Lausanne University and received his B.A. at Stanford University.

Other Books of Interest
from the Institute for the Study of Diplomacy and
University Press of America

CASE STUDIES IN DIPLOMACY

The Tokyo Round of Multilateral Trade Negotiations: A Case Study in Building Domestic Support for Diplomacy
by Joan E. Twiggs, with a Foreword by Robert S. Strauss

The Diplomacy of Human Rights
edited by David D. Newsom

U.N. Security Council Resolution 242: A Case Study in Diplomatic Ambiguity
by Lord Caradon, Arthur J. Goldberg, Mohamed El-Zayyat and Abba Eban

Resolution of the Dominican Crisis, 1965: A Study in Mediation
by Audrey Bracey, with concluding chapter by Martin F. Herz

Mediation of the West New Guinea Dispute, 1962: A Case Study
by Christopher J. McMullen, with Introduction by George C. McGhee

Resolution of the Yemen Crisis, 1963: A Case Study in Mediation
by Christopher J. McMullen

American Diplomats and the Franco-Prussian War: Perceptions from Paris and Berlin
by Patricia Dougherty, O.P.

Conference Diplomacy—A Case Study: The World Food Conference, Rome, 1974
by Edwin McC. Martin

Conference Diplomacy II—A Case Study: The UN Conference on Science and Technology for Development, Vienna, 1979
by Jean M. Wilkowski, with Foreword by John W. McDonald, Jr.

SYMPOSIA ON PROBLEMS AND PROCESSES OF DIPLOMACY

The Modern Ambassador: The Challenge and the Search
edited by Martin F. Herz, with Introduction by Ellsworth Bunker

Diplomats and Terrorists: What Works, What Doesn't—A Symposium
edited by Martin F. Herz

Contacts with the Opposition—A Symposium
edited by Martin F. Herz

The Role of Embassies in Promoting Business—A Symposium
edited by Martin F. Herz, with Overview by Theodore H. Moran

Diplomacy: The Role of the Wife—A Symposium
edited by Martin F. Herz

The Consular Dimension of Diplomacy—A Symposium
edited by Martin F. Herz

EXEMPLARY DIPLOMATIC REPORTING SERIES & OCCASIONAL PAPERS

David Bruce's "Long Telegram" of July 3, 1951
by Martin F. Herz

A View from Tehran: A Diplomatist Looks at the Shah's Regime in 1964
by Martin F. Herz

The North-South Dialogue and the United Nations
by John W. McDonald, Jr.

Making the World a Less Dangerous Place: Lessons Learned from a Career in Diplomacy
by Martin F. Herz

DIPLOMATIC AND CONTEMPORARY HISTORY

215 Days in the Life of an American Ambassador
by Martin F. Herz

First Line of Defense—Forty Years' Experiences of a Career Diplomat
by Martin F. Herz

The Vietnam War in Retrospect
by Martin F. Herz

U.S.—Soviet Summits: An Account of East-West Diplomacy at the Top, 1955-1985
by Gordon R. Weihmiller and Dusko Doder

INSTITUTE FOR THE STUDY OF DIPLOMACY

Hon. Ellsworth Bunker
Chairman (1978-1984)

Hon. Martin F. Herz
Director of Studies (1978-1983)

BOARD OF DIRECTORS

Hon. Edmund S. Muskie
Chairman

Dean Peter F. Krogh   Hon. George C. McGhee
Vice-Chairmen

Hon. Lucius D. Battle
Hon. Maurice M. Bernbaum
Hon. Winthrop G. Brown
Mrs. John Moors Cabot
Marshall B. Coyne
Hon. Thomas O. Enders
Hon. Joseph S. Farland
Hon. Kenneth Franzheim II
Hon. Parker T. Hart
Hon. Ulric Haynes, Jr.
Dr. Elisabeth K. Herz
Jim Hoagland
R. Michael Huffington
Hon. Carol C. Laise

Gloria Elliot Lemos
Hon. Alonzo L. McDonald
Hon. Robert S. McNamara
Robert R. Nathan
Hon. David C. Miller, Jr.
Dr. Edmund D. Pellegrino
Jane G. Pisano
Hon. John E. Reinhardt
Hon. Abraham Ribicoff
Hon. Kenneth Rush
Smith Simpson
Hon. Gerard C. Smith
Hon. John Wills Tuthill
Hon. Charles S. Whitehouse

Hon. David D. Newsom
Director

Hon. Harold E. Horan
Director of Programs

Margery R. Boichel
Editor

Private Diplomacy with the Soviet Union
David D. Newsom, Editor

Private exchanges between the citizens of the United States and the Soviet Union, though often overlooked, represent a significant part of the relations between the two superpowers. This volume examines the extent to which these exchanges give signals to the two governments and thereby affect their basic political relationship and policies.

The authors—corporate and private association executives, scholars, and former ambassadors—explore questions often raised concerning nonofficial "diplomacy." Who gains in such exchanges? Indeed, why are the citizens of each country interested in such meetings: To "plug into ruling circles"? To seek channels of persuasion? Of information? Are there dangers of manipulation and disinformation? What special cultural, psychological or human relations obstacles arise?

The authors analyze, each from a different perspective, the value of private exchanges to the official Soviet-American dialogue and spell out useful lessons learned.

"The underlying purpose of this dialogue, in most cases, is to reach understanding, to eliminate areas of ignorance, to overcome stereotypes, to establish a process of ongoing communication. . . . This cannot be achieved by wishful or sentimental thinking or pretty words. . . . It is necessary that a person be open and forthcoming, and that involves risks."
—Landrum R. Bolling
Subjective Reflections on the Dartmouth Conference

"We businessmen must leave to the statesmen the enormous and delicate tasks related to the art of diplomatic give-and-take. . . . But in our own way, when the opportunity arises, we can make positive contributions to the process through our established bonds of mutual interest, just as long as these efforts do not infringe on sensitive negotiations related to national policy issues."
—Armand Hammer
Private Diplomacy at the Highest Levels

"The Soviets never seem fully to understand the difference between official and private individuals and are continually looking to businessmen to provide clues to U.S. policy or to influence such policy. . . . One must be constantly alert to avoid legitimate misunderstandings. . . . Nevertheless, while they are proud, hard bargainers, it is possible to do business with them, to sign binding agreements that are mutually beneficial, and to make a profit."
—Robert D. Schmidt
Business Negotiations with the Soviet Union

"When the Soviets and Americans meet each other, there will be an extraordinary amount of creative tension. There will be guilt, there will be dreams, there will be suspicion. Above all, perhaps, there will be hope."
—James L. Hickman and James A. Garrison, Jr.
Psychological Principles of Citizen Diplomacy

0-8191-5821-6